Simply Natural

Authentic recipes for the whole-food cook

Real Food For Real Life

Vegan **Vegetarian** **Raw** **Dairy-free** **Gluten-free**

With its powerful performance and ultra-responsive controls, the Vitamix 7500 will completely change your perception of what a blender can do. Easily create healthy, delicious meals from fresh, whole-food ingredients, and discover why Vitamix is the most trusted brand among professional chefs.

The quality and versatility of your Vitamix 7500 will help you create every possible texture, from chunky nut butters to silky-smooth purées, while it replaces several other kitchen tools. With a Vitamix machine, you can chop, cream, blend, heat, grind, churn, emulsify, crush, whisk, frappé, purée, powder, and whip through every course of every meal.

Enjoy this collection of recipes, specially developed for the Vitamix 7500, and then begin to explore your own creative inventions. *Simply Natural* is all about maximizing the power of your Vitamix 7500 to help you save time and create exquisite meals to enjoy with family and friends. With Vitamix, every meal is easier, healthier, and more delicious!

Simply Natural features five icons that will allow you to easily identify recipes based on your dietary interests. Pictured above, these icons can be found throughout the book as well as listed in the index for quick searching.

For more recipes and inspiration, visit **vitamix.com**.

Beverages

Vegan

Vegetarian

Raw

Dairy-free

Gluten-free

From nutrition-packed breakfast smoothies and juices to homemade dairy-free milks, these recipes will show you how to expertly prepare delicious beverages in your Vitamix machine.

Beverages

SMOOTHIES / JUICES / COFFEES / MILKS

Blackberry Pear Smoothie

Preparation: 10 minutes | **Processing:** 30 seconds
Yield: 4 ¾ cups (1.1 l) (4 servings)

1 cup (245 g) plain unsweetened soy yogurt

⅔ cup (160 ml) water

2 bananas, peeled

1 ripe pear, 7 ounces (200 g), halved and cored

2 cups (280 g) frozen unsweetened blackberries

1. Place all ingredients into the Vitamix container in the order listed and secure lid.

2. Select Variable 1.

3. Switch machine to Start and slowly increase speed to Variable 10.

4. Blend for 30 seconds or until desired consistency is reached, using the tamper to press the ingredients into the blades.

Nutritional Information

Amount Per Serving: *Calories 130, Total Fat 1.5g, Saturated Fat 0g, Cholesterol 0mg, Sodium 5mg, Total Carbohydrate 30g, Dietary Fiber 6g, Sugars 19g, Protein 3g*

Vegan   **Vegetarian**   **Dairy-free**   **Gluten-free**

Create Your Own

Fun Pops

Smoothies can easily be turned into delicious frozen pops, providing another fun way for kids to enjoy their fruits, veggies, and greens.

Pour any prepared smoothie into ice pop molds (small paper cups will also work) and freeze until almost solid. Insert wooden craft sticks into each pop so the sticks stand upright. Return to the freezer until completely solid. To remove pops, run a little warm water over the bottom to loosen them from the mold.

Play with texture by adding a few fresh berries, or layer two to three different smoothies in the mold for fun color and flavor variety.

Pomegranate Berry Smoothie

Preparation: 10 minutes | **Processing:** 45 seconds
Yield: 3 ¾ cups (900 ml) (3 servings)

½ cup (120 ml) water

1 cup (240 ml) pomegranate juice

½ cup (113 g) low-fat cottage cheese

½ banana, peeled

2 cups (280 g) frozen unsweetened mixed berries

1. Place all ingredients into the Vitamix container in the order listed and secure lid.

2. Select Variable 1.

3. Switch machine to Start and slowly increase speed to Variable 10.

4. Blend for 45 seconds or until desired consistency is reached.

Nutritional Information

Amount Per Serving: *Calories 140, Total Fat 1.5g, Saturated Fat 0g, Cholesterol 5mg, Sodium 135mg, Total Carbohydrate 29g, Dietary Fiber 3g, Sugars 22g, Protein 6g*

Vegetarian

Gluten-free

Spiced Banana Yogurt Smoothie

Preparation: 10 minutes | ***Processing:*** 20–30 seconds
Yield: 4 cups (960 ml) (4 servings)

2 cups (490 g) plain unsweetened soy yogurt

2 ripe bananas, peeled and halved

½ teaspoon ground cinnamon

⅛ teaspoon ground allspice

⅛ teaspoon ground nutmeg

1 cup (240 ml) ice cubes

1. Place all ingredients into the Vitamix container in the order listed and secure lid.

2. Select Variable 1.

3. Switch machine to Start and slowly increase speed to Variable 10.

4. Blend for 20 to 30 seconds or until desired consistency is reached.

Nutritional Information

Amount Per Serving: *Calories 120, Total Fat 3g, Saturated Fat 0.5g, Cholesterol 0mg, Sodium 15mg, Total Carbohydrate 17g, Dietary Fiber 3g, Sugars 8g, Protein 6g*

 Vegan **Vegetarian** **Dairy-free** **Gluten-free**

Raspberry Peach Smoothie

Preparation: 10 minutes | **Processing:** 45 seconds
Yield: 4 ¼ cups (1.0 l) (4 servings)

¾ cup (180 ml) water

2 ½ cups (375 g) grapes

2 Tablespoons (30 ml) honey (optional)

2 cups (300 g) frozen unsweetened peach slices

1 cup (150 g) frozen unsweetened raspberries

1. Place all ingredients into the Vitamix container in the order listed and secure lid.

2. Select Variable 1.

3. Switch machine to Start and slowly increase speed to Variable 10.

4. Blend for 45 seconds or until desired consistency is reached, using the tamper to press the ingredients into the blades.

Nutritional Information

Amount Per Serving: *Calories 140, Total Fat 0g, Saturated Fat 0g, Cholesterol 0mg, Sodium 0mg, Total Carbohydrate 36g, Dietary Fiber 3g, Sugars 30g, Protein 1g*

Vegetarian **Dairy-free** **Gluten-free**

Chef's Note

For a raw *or vegan smoothie, simply omit the honey in this recipe.*

Ingredient IQ

Produce at its Peak

Fresh produce tastes best — and has the most nutrients — when grown, picked, and served at its peak. You'll find the freshest at your local farmer's market. Growing seasons differ by region, but here are some seasonal highlights:

Winter: citrus fruits

Spring: pineapple, strawberries

Summer: melons, raspberries, blackberries, blueberries, peaches, apricots, nectarines, kiwi

Fall: pears, apples

Peach Cobbler Smoothie

Preparation: 10 minutes | ***Processing:*** 40–45 seconds | ***Yield:*** 4 ½ cups (1.0 l) (4 servings)

¾ cup (180 ml) peach nectar

2 cups (480 g) vanilla yogurt

1 teaspoon vanilla extract

1 teaspoon honey

½ teaspoon ground nutmeg

2 teaspoons wheat germ

4 teaspoons uncooked rolled oats

2 cups (300 g) frozen unsweetened peach slices

1 cup (240 ml) ice cubes

1. Place all ingredients into the Vitamix container in the order listed and secure lid.

2. Select Variable 1.

3. Switch machine to Start and slowly increase speed to Variable 10.

4. Blend for 40 to 45 seconds or until desired consistency is reached, using the tamper to press the ingredients into the blades.

Nutritional Information

Amount Per Serving: *Calories 160, Total Fat 1.5g, Saturated Fat 1g, Cholesterol 5mg, Sodium 75mg, Total Carbohydrate 30g, Dietary Fiber 2g, Sugars 22g, Protein 6g*

Vegetarian

Apple Pie Smoothie

Preparation: 10 minutes | **Processing:** 40 seconds | **Yield:** 3 cups (720 ml) (3 servings)

¾ cup (180 g) low-fat vanilla yogurt

11 ½ ounces (327 g) apples, quartered and cored

½ teaspoon apple pie spice

1 Tablespoon brown sugar

2 cups (480 ml) ice cubes

1. Place all ingredients into the Vitamix container in the order listed and secure lid.

2. Select Variable 1.

3. Switch machine to Start and slowly increase speed to Variable 10.

4. Blend for 40 seconds or until desired consistency is reached, using the tamper to press the ingredients into the blades.

Nutritional Information

Amount Per Serving: *Calories 130, Total Fat 1g, Saturated Fat 0.5g, Cholesterol 5mg, Sodium 50mg, Total Carbohydrate 28g, Dietary Fiber 3g, Sugars 24g, Protein 3g*

Vegetarian **Gluten-free**

Fruit Salad Smoothie

Preparation: 20 minutes | **Processing:** 30–40 seconds
Yield: 4 ¼ cups (1.0 l) (4 servings)

½ cup (75 g) green grapes

1 medium orange, peeled
and halved

½-inch-thick (1.3 cm) slice
pineapple, core included, halved

½ cup (65 g) peeled and
chopped cucumber

1 medium carrot, 2 ½ ounces
(71 g), halved

1 medium apple, 6 ounces
(170 g), quartered and seeded

2 ½ cups (600 ml) ice cubes

1. Place all ingredients into the Vitamix container in the order
   listed and secure lid.

2. Select Variable 1.

3. Switch machine to Start and slowly increase speed to Variable 10.

4. Blend for 30 to 40 seconds or until desired consistency is reached,
   using the tamper to press the ingredients into the blades.

Nutritional Information

Amount Per Serving: *Calories 70, Total Fat 0g, Saturated Fat 0g, Cholesterol 0mg,
Sodium 20mg, Total Carbohydrate 19g, Dietary Fiber 3g, Sugars 14g, Protein 1g*

Vegan **Vegetarian** **Raw** **Dairy-free** **Gluten-free**

Blueberry Pineapple Smoothie

Preparation: 15 minutes | **Processing:** 30 – 40 seconds
Yield: 2 ½ cups (600 ml) (2 servings)

¼ cup (60 ml) orange juice

¼ cup (60 ml) pineapple juice

½ cup (120 g) low-fat
vanilla yogurt

1 banana, peeled

2 cups (60 g) fresh spinach
leaves, lightly packed

1 cup (140 g) frozen
unsweetened blueberries

¼ cup (35 g) frozen dark
sweet cherries

½ cup (120 ml) ice cubes

1. Place all ingredients into the Vitamix container in the order listed and secure lid.

2. Select Variable 1.

3. Switch machine to Start and slowly increase speed to Variable 10.

4. Blend for 30 to 40 seconds or until desired consistency is reached.

Nutritional Information

Amount Per Serving: *Calories 190, Total Fat 1.5g, Saturated Fat 0.5g, Cholesterol 5mg, Sodium 85mg, Total Carbohydrate 43g, Dietary Fiber 5g, Sugars 30g, Protein 5g*

Vegetarian **Gluten-free**

Buying Organic

There are many benefits to buying organic produce — not just for your health, but for the health of the environment as well. By purchasing organic, you're supporting small-scale farmers and eliminating exposure to pesticides for both yourself and wildlife. You're also protecting water supply, as pesticides can contaminate groundwater.

Leafy greens, grapes, blueberries, apples, peaches, and cucumbers are just a few of the items that should always be purchased organic. These foods, coined the "Dirty Dozen," are updated yearly, so make sure you're aware of any items added to the list.

Tropical Sailing Smoothie

Preparation: 10 minutes | **Processing:** 20–30 seconds
Yield: 3 ¾ cups (900 ml) (3 servings)

1 cup (240 ml) orange juice

1 cup (240 g) low-fat vanilla yogurt

1 banana, peeled

1 ⅓ cups (250 g) frozen unsweetened pineapple chunks

1. Place all ingredients into the Vitamix container in the order listed and secure lid.

2. Select Variable 1.

3. Switch machine to Start and slowly increase speed to Variable 10.

4. Blend for 20 to 30 seconds or until desired consistency is reached.

Nutritional Information

Amount Per Serving: *Calories 190, Total Fat 1.5g, Saturated Fat 0.5g, Cholesterol 5mg, Sodium 55mg, Total Carbohydrate 40g, Dietary Fiber 2g, Sugars 25g, Protein 6g*

Vegetarian   Gluten-free

Chef's Note

To reduce the *sweetness of this recipe, use plain or Greek yogurt instead of vanilla.*

Burst of Berries Smoothie

Preparation: 10 minutes | **Processing:** 45 seconds
Yield: 2 ½ cups (600 ml) (2 servings)

½ cup (120 ml) orange juice

½ cup (120 g) strawberry yogurt

½ cup (72 g) fresh strawberries

1 cup (140 g) frozen unsweetened blackberries

1 cup (140 g) frozen unsweetened blueberries

½ cup (120 ml) ice cubes

1. Place all ingredients into the Vitamix container in the order
   listed and secure lid.

2. Select Variable 1.

3. Switch machine to Start and slowly increase speed to Variable 10.

4. Blend for 45 seconds or until desired consistency is reached,
   using the tamper to press the ingredients into the blades.

Nutritional Information

Amount Per Serving: *Calories 180, Total Fat 1.5g, Saturated Fat 0g, Cholesterol 5mg,
Sodium 40mg, Total Carbohydrate 41g, Dietary Fiber 6g, Sugars 30g, Protein 4g*

Vegetarian **Gluten-free**

Berry Grape Smoothie

Preparation: 10 minutes | **Processing:** 45 seconds
Yield: 4 cups (960 ml) (4 servings)

1 cup (240 ml) water

2 cups (300 g) red grapes

1 cup (150 g) frozen unsweetened strawberries

1 cup (150 g) frozen unsweetened blueberries

2 cups (240 g) frozen unsweetened raspberries

1. Place all ingredients into the Vitamix container in the order listed and secure lid.

2. Select Variable 1.

3. Switch machine to Start and slowly increase speed to Variable 10.

4. Blend for 45 seconds or until desired consistency is reached, using the tamper to press the ingredients into the blades.

Nutritional Information

Amount Per Serving: *Calories 90, Total Fat 0g, Saturated Fat 0g, Cholesterol 0mg, Sodium 0mg, Total Carbohydrate 25g, Dietary Fiber 4g, Sugars 17g, Protein 1g*

Vegan   **Vegetarian**   **Raw**   **Dairy-free**   **Gluten-free**

Chef's Note

The vibrant color of this smoothie makes it a perfect recipe when hosting a shower or brunch. Prepare a glass of the original recipe for each of your guests, and stir in sparkling water or champagne for a bubbly spritzer.

Cherry Berry Smoothie

Preparation: 15 minutes | *Processing:* 30–40 seconds | *Yield:* 3 cups (720 ml) (3 servings)

1 cup (240 ml) pomegranate juice

6 ounces (170 g) fresh strawberries

½ cup (74 g) fresh blueberries

1 cup (123 g) fresh raspberries

1 cup (140 g) frozen dark sweet cherries

1. Place all ingredients into the Vitamix container in the order listed and secure lid.

2. Select Variable 1.

3. Switch machine to Start and slowly increase speed to Variable 10.

4. Blend for 30 to 40 seconds or until desired consistency is reached.

Nutritional Information

Amount Per Serving: Calories 130, Total Fat 0.5g, Saturated Fat 0g, Cholesterol 0mg, Sodium 10mg, Total Carbohydrate 31g, Dietary Fiber 5g, Sugars 24 g, Protein 2g

Vegan **Vegetarian** **Dairy-free** **Gluten-free**

Orange Flax Smoothie

Preparation: 15 minutes | **Processing:** 40 seconds
Yield: 3 cups (720 ml) (3 servings)

1 cup (240 ml) carrot juice

½ cup (120 ml) orange juice

2 Tablespoons (13 g) ground flaxseed

1 Tablespoon chopped fresh ginger root

2 cups (280 g) frozen unsweetened peach slices

1. Place all ingredients into the Vitamix container in the order listed and secure lid.

2. Select Variable 1.

3. Switch machine to Start and slowly increase speed to Variable 8.

4. Blend for 40 seconds or until desired consistency is reached.

Nutritional Information

Amount Per Serving: *Calories 100, Total Fat 1.5g, Saturated Fat 0g, Cholesterol 0mg, Sodium 20mg, Total Carbohydrate 21g, Dietary Fiber 3g, Sugars 15g, Protein 3g*

Vegan **Vegetarian** **Dairy-free** **Gluten-free**

Ingredient IQ

Using Flaxseed

Rich in omega-3 fatty acids and fiber, flaxseed is a great addition to your diet. To reap its nutritional benefits, flaxseed must be ground or milled to produce flaxseed meal, which can then be added to smoothies, baked goods, sauces, or sprinkled over salads.

Because of its sensitivity to oxidation, it's best to grind flaxseed as you need it, or store excess flaxseed meal refrigerated in an airtight container.

Frozen Strawberry Grape Smoothie

Preparation: 10 minutes | **Processing:** 30 seconds | **Yield:** 2 ½ cups (600 ml) (2 servings)

1 cup (150 g) green grapes

1 cup (150 g) red grapes

1 cup (150 g) frozen unsweetened strawberries

½ cup (120 ml) ice cubes

1. Place all ingredients into the Vitamix container in the order listed and secure lid.

2. Select Variable 1.

3. Switch machine to Start and slowly increase speed to Variable 10.

4. Blend for 30 seconds or until desired consistency is reached, using the tamper to press the ingredients into the blades.

Nutritional Information

Amount Per Serving: *Calories 130, Total Fat 0g, Saturated Fat 0g, Cholesterol 0mg, Sodium 0mg, Total Carbohydrate 34g, Dietary Fiber 3g, Sugars 26g, Protein 2g*

Vegan   **Vegetarian**   **Raw**   **Dairy-free**   **Gluten-free**

Green Tea Smoothie

Preparation: 15 minutes | ***Processing:*** 30–40 seconds
Yield: 4 ½ cups (1.0 l) (4 servings)

1 ¾ cups (420 ml) strong brewed green tea, hot

1 Hass avocado, 8 ounces (227 g), halved, pitted, and peeled

2 teaspoons honey

2 cups (60 g) fresh spinach leaves, lightly packed

3 cups (560 g) frozen unsweetened green grapes

1 cup (240 ml) ice cubes

1. Place all ingredients into the Vitamix container in the order listed and secure lid.

2. Select Variable 1.

3. Switch machine to Start and slowly increase speed to Variable 10.

4. Blend for 30 to 40 seconds or until desired consistency is reached.

Nutritional Information

Amount Per Serving: *Calories 200, Total Fat 9g, Saturated Fat 1g, Cholesterol 0mg, Sodium 40mg, Total Carbohydrate 32g, Dietary Fiber 5g, Sugars 23g, Protein 1g*

Vegetarian **Dairy-free** **Gluten-free**

Spring Green Smoothie

Preparation: 15 minutes | **Processing:** 45 seconds
Yield: 4 ¾ cups (1.1 l) (4 servings)

¼ cup (60 ml) water

1 ½ cups (225 g) green grapes

1 orange, peeled and halved

½ lemon, peeled

½ cucumber, cut into
large chunks

½ green apple, 3 ½ ounces
(99 g), halved and seeded

1 cup (67 g) kale,
spine removed

1 cup (50 g) romaine lettuce

1 cup (60 g) parsley leaves

1 cup (150 g)
frozen unsweetened
pineapple chunks

2 cups (480 ml) ice cubes

1. Place all ingredients into the Vitamix container in the order
   listed and secure lid.

2. Select Variable 1.

3. Switch machine to Start and slowly increase speed to Variable 10.

4. Blend for 45 seconds or until desired consistency is reached.

Nutritional Information

Amount Per Serving: *Calories 90, Total Fat 0g, Saturated Fat 0g,
Cholesterol 0mg, Sodium 15mg, Total Carbohydrate 21g,
Dietary Fiber 3g, Sugars 13g, Protein 2g*

 Vegan   **Vegetarian**   **Raw**   **Dairy-free**   **Gluten-free**

The Riper the Better

Most often when we're
shopping for fruit, we look
for slightly green produce so
it doesn't spoil before we're
able to use it. For this recipe,
however, the riper the apples
and oranges, the sweeter
the smoothie. The added
benefit is that riper fruits
and vegetables are also
more nutritious.

Green fruits should be stored
at room temperature for a
few days until they're fully
ripened. Always store
leafy greens such as kale
and romaine lettuce in the
refrigerator to maintain
freshness.

Garden Green Smoothie

Preparation: 20 minutes | **Processing:** 40 seconds
Yield: 4 ¼ cups (1.0 l) (4 servings)

¼ cup (60 ml) water

1 cup (150 g) green grapes

1 orange, 4 ½ ounces
(128 g), peeled and halved

½ celery stalk, 1 ounce
(28 g), halved

½ small carrot, 1 ounce
(28 g), halved

1 green apple, 6 ½ ounces
(185 g), cored and quartered

½ medium zucchini,
3 ½ ounces (100 g),
cut into large chunks

1 cup (50 g) romaine lettuce

1 cup (67 g) kale,
spine removed

½ cup (30 g) parsley leaves

2 cups (480 ml) ice cubes

1. Place all ingredients into the Vitamix container in the order listed and secure lid.

2. Select Variable 1.

3. Switch machine to Start and slowly increase speed to Variable 10.

4. Blend for 40 seconds or until desired consistency is reached, using the tamper to press the ingredients into the blades.

Nutritional Information

Amount Per Serving: *Calories 80, Total Fat 0g, Saturated Fat 0g, Cholesterol 0mg, Sodium 25mg, Total Carbohydrate 19g, Dietary Fiber 3g, Sugars 14g, Protein 2g*

Vegan **Vegetarian** **Raw** **Dairy-free** **Gluten-free**

Minty Green Smoothie

Preparation: 10 minutes | **Processing:** 30 – 40 seconds
Yield: 3 ½ cups (840 ml) (3 servings)

1 cup (240 ml) water

4 cups (120 g) fresh spinach leaves

4 small mint leaves

2 ½ cups (375 g) fresh pineapple chunks

1 ½ cups (360 ml) ice cubes

1. Place all ingredients into the Vitamix container in the order
   listed and secure lid.

2. Select Variable 1.

3. Switch machine to Start and slowly increase speed to Variable 10.

4. Blend for 30 to 40 seconds or until desired consistency is reached.

Nutritional Information

Amount Per Serving: Calories 80, Total Fat 0g, Saturated Fat 0g, Cholesterol 0mg,
Sodium 65mg, Total Carbohydrate 20g, Dietary Fiber 2g, Sugars 11g, Protein 2g

Vegan **Vegetarian** **Raw** **Dairy-free** **Gluten-free**

Green Pick Me Up Smoothie

Preparation: 10 minutes | ***Processing:*** 30 seconds
Yield: 2 ½ cups (600 ml) (2 servings)

½ cup (75 g) green grapes

½ orange, peeled

½ green apple, seeded

2 cups (72 g) Swiss chard

2 cups (480 ml) ice cubes

1. Place all ingredients into the Vitamix container in the order listed and secure lid.

2. Select Variable 1.

3. Switch machine to Start and slowly increase speed to Variable 10.

4. Blend for 30 seconds or until desired consistency is reached, using the tamper to press the ingredients into the blades.

Nutritional Information

Amount Per Serving: *Calories 70, Total Fat 0g, Saturated Fat 0g, Cholesterol 0mg, Sodium 85mg, Total Carbohydrate 18g, Dietary Fiber 3g, Sugars 14g, Protein 1g*

Vegan   **Vegetarian**   **Raw**   **Dairy-free**   **Gluten-free**

The Right Tools

Once you have your Vitamix and ingredients ready, your smoothies almost make themselves. Many of our recipes call for unpeeled fruit, but when needed, it's nice to be prepared with the right tools. Here are a few kitchen items that speed up food prep:

Vegetable peeler: These handheld swivel-bladed peelers make it quick to peel apples, carrots, cucumbers, and potatoes. They're sold in right- and left-handed models. Also look for padded grips for maximum comfort.

Chef's knife: These large knives are perfect for chopping fresh herbs and slicing fruits and vegetables. Keep yours sharp for the best (and safest) results.

Apple corer: Shaped like a vegetable peeler, but with a hollow round blade instead of the swivel blade, this tool easily removes cores and seeds from apples, pears, and tomatoes.

Going Green Smoothie

Preparation: 10 minutes | **Processing:** 40 seconds | **Yield:** 2 ½ cups (600 ml) (2 servings)

½ cup (120 ml) water

1 cup (150 g) green grapes

½ cup (75 g) fresh pineapple chunks, core included

½ banana, peeled

2 cups (60 g) fresh spinach, lightly packed

½ cup (120 ml) ice cubes

1. Place all ingredients into the Vitamix container in the order listed and secure lid.

2. Select Variable 1.

3. Switch machine to Start and slowly increase speed to Variable 10.

4. Blend for 40 seconds or until desired consistency is reached.

Nutritional Information

Amount Per Serving: *Calories 110, Total Fat 0g, Saturated Fat 0g, Cholesterol 0mg, Sodium 50mg, Total Carbohydrate 28g, Dietary Fiber 3g, Sugars 19g, Protein 2g*

Vegan

Vegetarian

Raw

Dairy-free

Gluten-free

Fresh Lemonade

Preparation: 10 minutes | **Processing:** 30 seconds
Yield: 3 cups (720 ml) (3 servings)

2 cups (480 ml) water

1 whole lemon, peeled with
1-inch (2.5 cm) strip of peel remaining

2 Tablespoons (30 ml) honey

1 cup (240 ml) ice cubes

1. Place all ingredients into the Vitamix container in the order listed and secure lid.

2. Select Variable 1.

3. Switch machine to Start and slowly increase speed to Variable 10.

4. Blend for 30 seconds or until desired consistency is reached.

Nutritional Information

Per 240 ml (1 cup) Serving: *Calories 50, Total Fat 0g, Saturated Fat 0g, Cholesterol 0mg, Sodium 10mg, Total Carbohydrate 13g, Dietary Fiber 1g, Sugars 11g, Protein 0g*

Vegetarian   **Dairy-free**   **Gluten-free**

Make It Your Own

Flavored Lemonade

Play up the flavor of your homemade lemonade by adding fresh fruit or even herbs. Crushed berries such as strawberries, raspberries, and blueberries lend sweetness to the tart and tangy lemon. A sprig of fresh thyme or some muddled mint make refreshing flavor add-ins to a cold glass of lemonade.

The same works for flavoring water; adding fresh, all-natural fruits, vegetables, or herbs can help you increase your water intake while avoiding sugary beverages from concentrate. Experiment with flavor combinations like sliced cucumber with lemon, or infuse your water with herbs such as basil and lemongrass.

Another way you can add variety to your beverages is with flavored ice cubes. Simply add crushed herbs or berries to an ice cube tray, cover with water, and freeze. A flavor boost to your beverage will be as simple as adding ice.

Garden Fresh Cocktail

Preparation: 15 minutes | *Processing:* 30 seconds | *Yield:* 2 ⅔ cups (640 ml) (2 servings)

8 ounces (227 g) ripe tomato, quartered	½ red or green bell pepper, 3 ½ ounces (99 g)
½ cup (15 g) fresh spinach, lightly packed	⅛ teaspoon hot sauce
½ carrot, 1 ounce (28 g)	½ teaspoon Worcestershire sauce
½ ounce (14 g) onion	Dash of salt
1 sprig parsley	1 cup (240 ml) ice cubes

1. Place all ingredients into the Vitamix container in the order listed and secure lid.

2. Select Variable 1.

3. Switch machine to Start and slowly increase speed to Variable 10.

4. Blend for 30 seconds or until desired consistency is reached.

Nutritional Information

Amount Per Serving: Calories 50, Total Fat 0g, Saturated Fat 0g, Cholesterol 0mg, Sodium 50mg, Total Carbohydrate 10g, Dietary Fiber 3g, Sugars 6g, Protein 2g

Dairy-free   Gluten-free

Lime and Mint Agua Fresca

Preparation: 15 minutes | ***Processing:*** 20 – 30 seconds | ***Yield:*** 2 ¾ cups (660 ml) (2 servings)

1 ½ cups (360 ml) water

1 Tablespoon honey

1 ¾ cups (298 g)
honeydew chunks

1 ½ cups (200 g) cucumber,
peeled and cut into
large chunks

½ lime, peeled

2 Tablespoons (11 g)
fresh mint leaves

½ teaspoon lime zest

1 cup (240 ml) ice cubes

Mint sprigs, for garnish

1. Place water, honey, honeydew, cucumber, lime, spearmint leaves, zest, and ice into the Vitamix container in the order listed and secure lid.

2. Select Variable 1.

3. Switch machine to Start and slowly increase speed to Variable 10.

4. Blend for 20 to 30 seconds or until desired consistency is reached, using the tamper to press the ingredients into the blades.

5. Pour into glasses and garnish with mint sprig.

Nutritional Information

Amount Per Serving: *Calories 70, Total Fat 0g, Saturated Fat 0g, Cholesterol 0mg, Sodium 30mg, Total Carbohydrate 18g, Dietary Fiber 2g, Sugars 15g, Protein 1g*

Vegetarian   **Dairy-free**   **Gluten-free**

Apple Beet Juice

Preparation: 15 minutes | *Processing:* 1 minute | *Yield:* 5 ½ cups (1.3 l) (5 ½ servings)

2 cups (480 ml) apple juice

9 ½ ounces (270 g) raw beets, skin on, scrubbed, and cut into pieces

2 medium carrots, 4 ½ ounces (128 g), skin on, scrubbed, and cut into pieces

1 medium apple, 5 ounces (142 g), seeded and quartered

1 cup (40 g) loosely packed spinach

1 cup (240 ml) ice cubes

1. Place all ingredients into the Vitamix container in the order listed and secure lid.

2. Select Variable 1.

3. Switch machine to Start and slowly increase speed to Variable 10.

4. Blend for 1 minute or until desired consistency is reached.

Nutritional Information

Amount Per Serving: Calories 90, Total Fat 0g, Saturated Fat 0g, Cholesterol 0mg, Sodium 75mg, Total Carbohydrate 21g, Dietary Fiber 3g, Sugars 17g, Protein 1g

Vegan Vegetarian Dairy-free Gluten-free

Strawberry Agua Fresca

Preparation: 20 minutes | **Processing:** 30–40 seconds
Yield: 4 cups (960 ml) (4 servings)

4 cups (620 g) cubed and seeded watermelon

2 cups (300 g) fresh strawberries

2 Tablespoons (30 ml) fresh lemon juice

2 cups (480 ml) ice cubes

1. Place all ingredients into the Vitamix container in the order listed and secure lid.

2. Select Variable 1.

3. Switch machine to Start and slowly increase speed to Variable 10.

4. Blend for 30 to 40 seconds or until desired consistency is reached, using the tamper to press the ingredients into the blades.

Nutritional Information

Amount Per Serving: *Calories 60, Total Fat 0g, Saturated Fat 0g, Cholesterol 0mg, Sodium 10mg, Total Carbohydrate 20g, Dietary Fiber 2g, Sugars 16g, Protein 1g*

Vegan   **Vegetarian**   **Raw**   **Dairy-free**   **Gluten-free**

Apple Juice

Preparation: 10 minutes | ***Processing:*** 45 seconds
Yield: 1 cup (240 ml) strained (1 serving)

1 ½ pounds (680 g) apples, cored and quartered

⅓ cup (80 ml) cool water

Tools needed:

2 double layers of cheesecloth or filtration bag

1. Place apple and water into the Vitamix container in the order listed and secure lid.

2. Select Variable 1.

3. Switch machine to Start and slowly increase speed to Variable 10.

4. Blend for 45 seconds or until desired consistency is reached, using the tamper to press the ingredients into the blades.

5. Dampen cheesecloth or filtration bag and squeeze out excess moisture. Transfer purée to a bowl lined with cheesecloth or filtration bag and twist until juice is extracted.

Nutritional Information

Amount Per Serving: *Calories 120, Total Fat 0g, Saturated Fat 0g, Cholesterol 0mg, Sodium 25mg, Total Carbohydrate 30g, Dietary Fiber 0g, Sugars 26g, Protein 0g*

 Vegan
 Vegetarian
 Raw
 Dairy-free
Gluten-free

Healthy Choices

ABCs of Vitamin-Rich Fruits

Vitamins are essential for good health. Here's where those vitamins are found in your favorite fruits:

A: cantaloupes, grapefruits

B1: grapes, grapefruits, mangos, oranges, pineapples

B2: bananas, grapes, mangos, pomegranates

B3: mangos, nectarines, peaches

B6: bananas, dates, grapes, mangos, pineapples

C: oranges, grapefruits, kiwis, mangos, pineapples, strawberries, apples

E: blueberries, cranberries, guavas, mangos, nectarines, peaches, raspberries

K: blueberries, grapes, pears, plums, raspberries

Carrot Cider with Ginger

Preparation: 10 minutes | **Processing:** 30 seconds
Yield: 3 cups (720 ml) (3 servings)

2 cups (480 ml) apple cider or apple juice

6 ounces (170 g) carrots, halved, about 3 medium

½ teaspoon chopped fresh ginger root

1 cup (240 ml) ice cubes

1. Place all ingredients into the Vitamix container in the order listed and secure lid.

2. Select Variable 1.

3. Switch machine to Start and slowly increase speed to Variable 10.

4. Blend for 30 seconds or until desired consistency is reached, using the tamper to press the ingredients into the blades.

Nutritional Information

Amount Per Serving: Calories 100, Total Fat 0g, Saturated Fat 0g, Cholesterol 0mg, Sodium 55mg, Total Carbohydrate 25g, Dietary Fiber 2g, Sugars 20g, Protein 1g

Vegan **Vegetarian** **Dairy-free** **Gluten-free**

Ingredient IQ

A Flavorful Remedy

With its warm, zingy flavor, a little ginger goes a long way when added to food and beverages. In addition to the complexity it can bring to ordinary dishes, ginger boasts many nutritional and health benefits. It's known to aid in digestion and can soothe upset stomach and nausea. Ginger also contains anti-inflammatory properties, which can reduce pain and swelling associated with arthritis.

Ginger can be peeled and grated into certain foods, or blended into a smoothie or soup such as Thai Ginger Soup (See Soups).

Peeling ginger is simple, and because the skin is so thin, many people only need the side of a spoon to scrape away the outer layer.

Vanilla Coffee Frappé

Preparation: 15 minutes | **Processing:** 10 seconds
Yield: 2 ½ cups (600 ml) (2 servings)

1 cup (240 ml) espresso, cooled

½ cup (120 ml) half & half

3 Tablespoons (38 g) granulated sugar

1 ½ Tablespoons vanilla extract

1 ¼ cups (300 ml) ice cubes

1. Place all ingredients into the Vitamix container in the order listed and secure lid.

2. Select Variable 1.

3. Switch machine to Start and slowly increase speed to Variable 8.

4. Blend for 10 seconds or until desired consistency is reached.

Nutritional Information

Amount Per Serving: *Calories 190, Total Fat 7g, Saturated Fat 4.5g, Cholesterol 20mg, Sodium 45mg, Total Carbohydrate 25g, Dietary Fiber 0g, Sugars 20g, Protein 2g*

Vegetarian **Gluten-free**

Planning Ahead

Fix Your Morning Fix — Fast

On hot summer mornings, iced coffee drinks can be a real treat. You can still enjoy one, despite the got-to-get-to-work juggling, with a little bit of planning.

Fresh, cooled coffee is best in your Vanilla Coffee Frappé or other chilled coffee drinks, but since you don't often have time to wait for it to cool, simply place the brewed java in the freezer before you start your morning routine.

By the time you're dressed and ready, the coffee will be cold, but not frozen. Add ice and other ingredients when it's time to blend and you'll be out the door in no time.

Cappuccino

Preparation: 10 minutes | **Processing:** 10 seconds
Yield: 1 serving

¾ cup (180 ml) fresh brewed
double strength coffee or espresso

¼ cup (60 ml) milk, steamed

2 Tablespoons (30 g) white chocolate chips

¼ teaspoon vanilla extract

1. Place all ingredients into the Vitamix container in the order
   listed and secure lid.

2. Select Variable 1.

3. Switch machine to Start and slowly increase speed to Variable 8.

4. Blend for 10 seconds or until desired consistency is reached.

Nutritional Information

Amount Per Serving: *Calories 200, Total Fat 10g, Saturated Fat 8g, Cholesterol 5mg,
Sodium 85mg, Total Carbohydrate 25g, Dietary Fiber 0g, Sugars 21g, Protein 2g*

Vegetarian

Gluten-free

Chef's Note

For cold coffee *lovers,
try a Cappuccino or a
Pumpkin Latte over ice —
garnish with cinnamon
and crushed graham
crackers.*

Pumpkin Pie Latté

Preparation: 10 minutes | **Processing:** 20 seconds
Yield: 2 ½ cups (600 ml) (2 servings)

½ cup (120 ml) milk, steamed

1 ½ cups (360 ml) fresh brewed coffee

½ cup (120 ml) Pumpkin Spice Syrup (see sidebar)

1. Place all ingredients into the Vitamix container in the order listed and secure lid.

2. Select Variable 1.

3. Switch machine to Start and slowly increase speed to Variable 8.

4. Blend for 20 seconds or until desired consistency is reached.

Nutritional Information

Amount Per Serving: *Calories 90, Total Fat 2g, Saturated Fat 1g, Cholesterol 5mg, Sodium 35mg, Total Carbohydrate 16g, Dietary Fiber 1g, Sugars 15g, Protein 3g*

Vegetarian **Gluten-free**

Ingredient IQ

Pumpkin Spice Syrup

1 ¼ cups (300 ml) water

½ cup (120 g) pumpkin purée, fresh or canned

½ cup (100 g) granulated sugar

½ teaspoon vanilla extract

1 teaspoon ground cinnamon

½ teaspoon ground allspice

½ teaspoon ground ginger

1. Place all ingredients into the Vitamix container in the order listed and secure lid.

2. Select Variable 1.

3. Switch machine to Start and slowly increase speed to Variable 10.

4. Blend for 3 minutes or until mixture is thick and syrupy.

Mocha Spiced Coffee

Preparation: 10 minutes | **Processing:** 5 minutes
Yield: 2 cups (480 ml) (2 servings)

1 ½ cups (360 ml) milk

½ cup (90 g) semisweet chocolate chips

¼ teaspoon ground cinnamon

2 teaspoons instant espresso

⅛ teaspoon chili powder

1. Place all ingredients into the Vitamix container in the order listed and secure lid.

2. Select Variable 1.

3. Switch machine to Start and slowly increase speed to Variable 10.

4. Blend for 5 minutes or until heavy steam escapes from the vented lid plug.

Nutritional Information

Amount Per Serving: *Calories 400, Total Fat 22g, Saturated Fat 13g, Cholesterol 20mg, Sodium 80mg, Total Carbohydrate 46g, Dietary Fiber 3g, Sugars 41g, Protein 10g*

Vegetarian   Gluten-free

Chef's Note

Almond milk *is an excellent substitute for dairy milk and is available both sweetened and unsweetened. In this recipe, vanilla or chocolate-flavored almond milk works well. For a fresher, more indulgent Mocha Spiced Coffee, make your very own Almond Milk (see Beverages).*

Almond Milk

Preparation: 5 minutes plus overnight soaking
Processing: 45 seconds
Yield: 3 ½ cups (840 ml) (3 servings)

3 cups (720 ml) water

1 cup (140 g) raw almonds,
soaked overnight and drained

1. Place all ingredients into the Vitamix container in the order listed and secure lid.

2. Select Variable 1.

3. Switch machine to Start and slowly increase speed to Variable 10.

4. Blend for 45 seconds or until desired consistency is reached.

5. Store in refrigerator. Shake well before using.

Nutritional Information

Amount Per Serving: *Calories 270, Total Fat 24g, Saturated Fat 2g, Cholesterol 0mg, Sodium 10mg, Total Carbohydrate 10g, Dietary Fiber 6g, Sugars 1g, Protein 10g*

 Vegan   **Vegetarian**   **Raw**   **Dairy-free**   **Gluten-free**

Chef's Note

If you prefer *a touch of sweetness, add ½ teaspoon vanilla extract with the other ingredients; pure vanilla extract provides the best flavor.*

Bright Idea

Soaking Almonds

The benefits of soaking almonds are twofold; when using almonds to make Almond Milk, soaked almonds yield a smoother and more flavorful blend. Additionally, the nutritional value of almonds is maximized as it's easier for the body to digest almonds that have been soaked.

Simply place almonds in a large bowl and cover with 2 cups of purified water for every ½ cup of almonds. Allow the almonds to soak for at least four hours, if not overnight. If you don't plan on using them right away, the soaked almonds can be stored in plastic bags or jars and placed in the refrigerator for up to a week after soaking.

Rice Milk

Preparation: 45 minutes | **Processing:** 2 minutes 30 seconds – 3 minutes
Yield: 2 ½ cups (600 ml) (2 servings)

2 cups (480 ml) water

½ cup (100 g) cooked brown rice, cooled

½ Tablespoon honey, or to taste (optional)

1. Place all ingredients into the Vitamix container in the order
   listed and secure lid.

2. Select Variable 1.

3. Switch machine to Start and slowly increase speed to Variable 10.

4. Blend for 2 ½ to 3 minutes or until desired consistency is reached.

5. Store in refrigerator. Shake well before using.

Nutritional Information

Amount Per Serving: *Calories 60, Total Fat 0g, Saturated Fat 0g, Cholesterol 0mg,
Sodium 10mg, Total Carbohydrate 14g, Dietary Fiber 1g, Sugars 4g, Protein 1g*

Vegetarian Dairy-free Gluten-free

Coconut Milk

Preparation: 10 minutes | **Processing:** 3 minutes
Yield: 2 ½ cups (600 ml), unstrained (2 ½ servings)

2 cups (480 ml) water

1 cup (75 g) unsweetened,
shredded coconut

1. Place all ingredients into the Vitamix container in the order listed and secure lid.

2. Select Variable 1.

3. Switch machine to Start and slowly increase speed to Variable 10.

4. Blend for 3 minutes or until desired consistency is reached.

5. Store in refrigerator. Shake well before using.

Nutritional Information

Amount Per Serving: *Calories 260, Total Fat 23g, Saturated Fat 20g, Cholesterol 0mg, Sodium 20mg, Total Carbohydrate 9g, Dietary Fiber 4g, Sugars 2g, Protein 2g*

Vegan   Vegetarian   Dairy-free   Gluten-free

Soy Milk

Preparation: 8 hours | **Processing:** 1 minute
Cook Time: 15 minutes | **Yield:** 4 ¼ cups (1.0 l) (4 servings)

1 cup (200 g) dried soy beans

3 ½ cups (840 ml) water

1 Tablespoon honey (optional)

1. Clean dried soy beans and soak in water for 4 to 8 hours.
   Steam for about 15 minutes.

2. Drain soy beans and let cool. Measure 1 ½ cups (258 g) cooked beans.

3. Place cooked beans, water, and honey into the Vitamix container
   in the order listed and secure lid.

4. Select Variable 1.

5. Switch machine to Start and slowly increase speed to Variable 10.

6. Blend for 1 minute or until desired consistency is reached.

7. To obtain commercial-style soy milk, strain the milk through a
   filtration bag or pass through a fine mesh sieve.

Nutritional Information

Amount Per Serving: *Calories 130, Total Fat 6g, Saturated Fat 1g, Cholesterol 0mg,
Sodium 10mg, Total Carbohydrate 10g, Dietary Fiber 4g, Sugars 6g, Protein 11g*

Vegetarian **Dairy-free** **Gluten-free**

Chef's Note

For a refreshing flavor, *add a 1-inch (2.5 cm)
cube of ginger root
before blending.*

Cocktails

Vegan

Vegetarian

Dairy-free

Gluten-free

Whether you prefer *whole-fruit margaritas and daiquiris or a twist on classic drinks such as the Bloody Mary, the cocktails in this section provide plenty of options for entertaining guests.*

Cocktails

DAIQUIRIS / MARGARITAS / COCKTAILS

Cider and Whiskey Cocktail

Preparation: 10 minutes | **Processing:** 15 seconds
Yield: 2 cups (480 ml) 2 servings

½ cup (120 ml) fresh apple cider

2 ounces (60 ml) bourbon whiskey

1 Tablespoon real maple syrup

¼ small lemon, peeled

1 cup (240 ml) ice cubes

1. Place all ingredients into the Vitamix container in the order listed and secure lid.

2. Select Variable 1.

3. Switch machine to Start and slowly increase speed to Variable 5.

4. Blend for 15 seconds or until desired consistency is reached.

Nutritional Information

Amount Per Serving: Calories: 120, Total Fat: 0g, Saturated Fat: 0g, Cholesterol: 0g, Sodium 10mg, Total Carbohydrate 15g, Dietary Fiber 0g, Sugars 13g, Protein 0g

 Vegan   **Vegetarian**   **Dairy-free**

Ingredient IQ

Grading Maple Syrup

The use of maple syrup doesn't have to be limited to pancakes and waffles. In fact, it's often used as a sweetening agent in baking and cocktails, such as this Cider and Whisky Cocktail. When choosing maple syrup, be aware of its grade; depending on your taste preferences and what you're using it for, certain kinds of maple syrups work better than others.

Grade A Light Amber:
With a light, delicate flavor, this maple syrup is best used as a topping or cocktail mix-in.

Grade A Medium Amber:
Although this maple syrup has a full-bodied flavor that is slightly stronger than Grade A Light, it's still palatable enough to use in a cocktail or as a topping.

Grade A Dark Amber:
This maple syrup is best for cooking and baking as it has a deep, rich flavor and thick consistency.

Grade B: If you prefer a strong maple flavor, this grade of maple syrup is your best option. With its bold flavor and high viscosity, it's good for cooking and baking.

Peachy Keen Cocktail

Preparation: 15 minutes | ***Processing:*** Pulsing plus 30 seconds
Yield: 5 ½ cups (1.3 l) (5 servings)

½ cup (120 ml) orange juice

4 ounces (120 ml) light rum

6 ounces (170 g) thawed pink lemonade concentrate

3 fresh peaches, 10 ½ ounces (300 g), halved and pitted

3 cups (720 ml) ice cubes

1. Place orange juice, rum, concentrate, and peaches into the Vitamix container in the order listed and secure lid.

2. Select Variable 3.

3. Pulse 10 times.

4. Add ice to the Vitamix container and secure lid.

5. Select Variable 1.

6. Switch machine to Start and slowly increase speed to Variable 10.

7. Blend for 30 seconds or until desired consistency is reached.

Nutritional Information

Amount Per Serving: *Calories 150, Total Fat 0g, Saturated Fat 0g, Cholesterol 0mg, Sodium 0mg, Total Carbohydrate 25g, Dietary Fiber 1g, Sugars 18g, Protein 1g*

Vegan   **Vegetarian**   **Dairy-free**   **Gluten-free**

Strawberry Daiquiri

Preparation: 10 minutes | **Processing:** 30–40 seconds
Yield: 3 cups (720 ml) (3 servings)

4 ounces (120 ml) light rum

2 ounces (60 ml) triple sec

2 Tablespoons (30 ml) fresh lime juice

1 cup (150 g) frozen unsweetened strawberries, softened for 10 minutes

2–4 Tablespoons (16–32 g) powdered sugar

2 cups (480 ml) ice cubes

1. Place all ingredients into the Vitamix container in the order listed and secure lid.

2. Select Variable 1.

3. Switch machine to Start and slowly increase speed to Variable 8.

4. Blend for 30 to 40 seconds or until desired consistency is reached, using the tamper to press the ingredients into the blades.

Nutritional Information

Amount Per Serving: *Calories 190, Total Fat 0g, Saturated Fat 0g, Cholesterol 0mg, Sodium 0mg, Total Carbohydrate 18g, Dietary Fiber 1g, Sugars 14g, Protein 0g*

Vegan   **Vegetarian**   **Dairy-free**   **Gluten-free**

Play With Flavors

Flavored rums and vodkas are quite popular, and new ones are arriving on the market almost every day. Create your own zingy cocktails by substituting a flavorful infusion for standard rum or vodka.

Rums are available in lemon, lime, cherry, orange, raspberry, peach, and coconut flavors, to name a few. Vodkas really push the flavor envelope with pomegranate, mango, watermelon, chocolate, whipped cream, and bubble gum.

Chef's Note

The easiest way *to make simple syrup for the bar is to place equal parts of sugar and water into a sealed bottle and shake well. For thicker, more traditional syrup, you can then place the mixture in a pot and simmer over medium heat for 30 minutes.*

Blueberry Margarita

Preparation: 10 minutes | **Processing:** 25–30 seconds
Yield: 5 cups (1.2 l) (5 servings)

½ cup (120 ml) simple syrup

½ cup (120 ml) orange juice

¼ cup (60 ml) fresh lime juice

4 ounces (120 ml) tequila

½ cup (120 ml) blueberry juice

1 cup (148 g) fresh blueberries

4 cups (960 ml) ice cubes

1. Place all ingredients into the Vitamix container in the order listed and secure lid.

2. Select Variable 1.

3. Switch machine to Start and slowly increase speed to Variable 8.

4. Blend for 25 to 30 seconds or until desired consistency is reached.

Nutritional Information

Amount Per Serving: *Calories 280, Total Fat 0g, Saturated Fat 0g, Cholesterol 0mg, Sodium 10mg, Total Carbohydrate 57g, Dietary Fiber 1g, Sugars 54g, Protein 0g*

Vegan   **Vegetarian**   **Dairy-free**   **Gluten-free**

Pomarita Cocktail

Preparation: 10 minutes | ***Processing:*** 30 seconds | ***Yield:*** 3 cups (720 ml) (3 servings)

4 ounces (120 ml) tequila

1 cup (240 ml) 100% pomegranate juice

4 ounces (60 ml) triple sec

½ lime, peeled

2 Tablespoons (25 g) granulated sugar

2 cups (480 ml) ice cubes

1 fresh lime, thinly sliced

1. Place tequila, pomegranate juice, triple sec, lime, sugar, and ice cubes into the Vitamix container in the order listed and secure lid.

2. Select Variable 1.

3. Switch machine to Start and slowly increase speed to Variable 10.

4. Blend for 30 seconds or until desired consistency is reached.

5. Serve in a chilled cocktail glass and garnish each serving with one or two thin slices of fresh lime.

Nutritional Information

Amount Per Serving: *Calories 220, Total Fat 0g, Saturated Fat 0g, Cholesterol 0mg, Sodium 15mg, Total Carbohydrate 28g, Dietary Fiber 0g, Sugars 27g, Protein 0g*

Vegan   **Vegetarian**   **Dairy-free**   **Gluten-free**

Piña Colada

Preparation: 10 minutes | **Processing:** 40 seconds | **Yield:** 3 ½ cups (840 ml) (3 servings)

4 ½ ounces (135 ml) light rum

4 ½ Tablespoons (68 ml) cream of coconut

½ cup (120 ml) light coconut milk

2 Tablespoons (9 g) shredded coconut

¾ cup (100 g) fresh pineapple chunks, core included

3 cups (720 ml) ice cubes

1. Place all ingredients into the Vitamix container in the order listed and secure lid.

2. Select Variable 1.

3. Switch machine to Start and slowly increase speed to Variable 5.

4. Blend for 40 seconds or until desired consistency is reached.

Nutritional Information

Amount Per Serving: *Calories 260, Total Fat 9g, Saturated Fat 8g, Cholesterol 0mg, Sodium 30mg, Total Carbohydrate 23g, Dietary Fiber 0g, Sugars 20g, Protein 1g*

Vegan   Vegetarian   Dairy-free   Gluten-free

Islander Margarita

Preparation: 15 minutes | *Processing:* 1 minute | *Yield:* 1 serving

⅓ cup (80 ml) pineapple juice

1 ounce (30 ml) tequila

½ ounce triple sec

1 Tablespoon fresh lime juice

1 ½ teaspoons grenadine

½ cup (93 g) frozen unsweetened pineapple chunks, partially thawed

½ cup (93 g) frozen unsweetened mango chunks, partially thawed

1 cup (240 ml) ice cubes

1. Place all ingredients into the Vitamix container in the order listed and secure lid.

2. Select Variable 1.

3. Switch machine to Start and slowly increase speed to Variable 10.

4. Blend for 1 minute or until desired consistency is reached, using the tamper to press the ingredients into the blades.

Nutritional Information

Amount Per Serving: Calories 300, Total Fat 0g, Saturated Fat 0g, Cholesterol 0mg, Sodium 10mg, Total Carbohydrate 51g, Dietary Fiber 3g, Sugars 34g, Protein 1g

Vegan   **Vegetarian**   **Dairy-free**   **Gluten-free**

Whole Fruit Margarita

Preparation: 15 minutes | **Processing:** 40 seconds
Yield: 6 cups (1.4 l) (6 servings)

¼ cup (60 ml) water

6 ounces (180 ml) tequila

2 ounces (60 ml) Grand
Marnier or triple sec

1 medium orange,
peeled and halved

1 lime, peeled

1 lemon, peeled and halved

6 Tablespoons (75 g)
granulated sugar

6 cups (1.4 l) ice cubes

1. Place all ingredients into the Vitamix container in the order listed and secure lid.

2. Select Variable 1.

3. Switch machine to Start and slowly increase speed to Variable 10.

4. Blend for 40 seconds or until desired consistency is reached.

5. Pour into salt-rimmed margarita glasses.

Nutritional Information

Amount Per Serving: *Calories 150, Total Fat 0g, Saturated Fat 0g, Cholesterol 0mg, Sodium 10mg, Total Carbohydrate 20g, Dietary Fiber 1g, Sugars 18g, Protein 0g*

Vegan **Vegetarian** **Dairy-free** **Gluten-free**

Spicy Green Mary Cocktail

Preparation: 15 minutes | **Processing:** 30 seconds
Yield: 4 servings

6 ounces (180 ml) vodka

8 ounces (227 g) English cucumber,
cut into large chunks

2 Tablespoons (30 g) prepared horseradish

1 pound (454 g) tomatillos, husked, halved

⅛ teaspoon salt

1. Place all ingredients into the Vitamix container in the order listed and secure lid.

2. Select Variable 1.

3. Switch machine to Start and slowly increase speed to Variable 10.

4. Blend for 30 seconds or until desired consistency is reached.

5. Pour into ice-filled glasses and garnish.

Nutritional Information

Amount Per Serving: *Calories 150, Total Fat 1.5g, Saturated Fat 0g, Cholesterol 0mg, Sodium 105mg, Total Carbohydrate 10g, Dietary Fiber 3g, Sugars 6g, Protein 2g*

Vegan   Vegetarian   Dairy-free   Gluten-free

Frozen Bloody Mary

Preparation: 10 minutes plus 5 hours freeze time | ***Processing:*** Pulsing
Yield: 4 ½ cups (1.0 l) (4 servings)

3 cups (720 ml) tomato juice

1 cup (240 ml) beef broth

1 Tablespoon fresh lemon juice

1 teaspoon Worcestershire sauce

Few drops of hot sauce

4 ounces (120 ml) vodka

1. Combine tomato juice, beef broth, lemon juice, Worcestershire sauce, and hot sauce in a non-metal container. Cover and freeze for 5 hours.

2. Break up frozen mixture into large chunks.

3. Place into the Vitamix container, add vodka, and secure lid.

4. Select Variable 3.

5. Pulse a few times until slushy, using the tamper to press the ingredients into the blades.

Nutritional Information

Amount Per Serving: *Calories 120, Total Fat 0g, Saturated Fat 0g, Cholesterol 0mg, Sodium 740mg, Total Carbohydrate 9g, Dietary Fiber 1g, Sugars 6g, Protein 3g*

Dairy-free

Breakfasts

Vegan

Vegetarian

Raw

Dairy-free

Gluten-free

The most essential meal *of every day can be on the table in no time with your Vitamix machine. From smooth batter for pancakes and waffles, to fluffy egg mixtures for frittatas and quiches, a homemade breakfast brings everyone together.*

Breakfasts

BREADS / BATTERS / BAKES / BREAKFAST CONDIMENTS

Create Your Own Breakfast Bread

Preparation: 20 minutes | **Processing:** Pulsing plus 15 seconds
Bake Time: 55–60 minutes | **Yield:** 1 loaf (12 slices)

Chef's Note

This recipe makes it easy to modify ingredients to your exact specifications so you can create that perfect breakfast bread to enjoy with your morning coffee or tea. Simply choose your favorite combination of fruits or vegetables with the suggested mix-ins and follow the instructions listed.

Choose your fruit or vegetable:

2 medium apples, cored and quartered

1 medium firm pear, cored and quartered

1 medium zucchini, quartered

2 medium carrots, halved

Choose your mix-ins to equal 1 ¾ cups:

(limit to ¾ cup) walnuts, dried apricots, or dried cherries

(limit to ¾ cup) pecans, rolled oats, or pitted dates raisins or semisweet chocolate chips

(limit to ¾ cup) almonds or sweetened shredded coconut

Common ingredients:

1 ¼ cups (156 g) all-purpose flour

1 teaspoon baking powder

1 teaspoon salt

½ teaspoon baking soda

½ teaspoon ground cinnamon

½ teaspoon ground nutmeg

2 large eggs

½ cup (120 ml) light olive oil

½ cup (120 g) plain yogurt

1 teaspoon vanilla extract

1 teaspoon orange zest

¾ cup (150 g) granulated sugar

1. Preheat oven to 350°F (180°C). Lightly grease a 9-inch x 5-inch (23 cm x 13 cm) loaf pan.

2. If choosing apple or pear, place into the Vitamix container, fill with 3 cups (720 ml) water and secure lid.

3. Select Variable 7.

4. Pulse 8 to 10 times or until chopped. Drain well. Measure out 1 cup.

5. If choosing zucchini or carrot, place quartered sections into the Vitamix container and secure lid.

Create Your Own Breakfast Bread continues on page 82

continued from page 81

Create Your Own Breakfast Bread

6. Select Variable 7.

7. Pulse 8 to 10 times until chopped. Measure out 1 cup.

8. Measure and place selected mix-ins in a small bowl.

9. Place flour, baking powder, salt, baking soda, cinnamon, and nutmeg into a medium-size mixing bowl and stir by hand to combine. Stir in selected mix-ins.

10. Place 1 cup (150 g) fruit or vegetable, eggs, oil, yogurt, vanilla, orange zest, and sugar into the Vitamix container and secure lid.

11. Select Variable 1.

12. Switch machine to Start and slowly increase speed to Variable 5.

13. Blend for 15 seconds.

14. Pour wet mixture into dry ingredients and stir by hand to combine.

15. Pour into prepared loaf pan and bake 55 to 60 minutes or until a toothpick inserted into the center comes out clean. Cool in pan on wire rack for 30 minutes. Remove from pan and cool completely on wire rack.

Nutritional Information

Amount Per Slice (with apple, walnuts, oats and raisins): *Calories 280, Total Fat 15g, Saturated Fat 2g, Cholesterol 30mg, Sodium 310mg, Total Carbohydrate 33g, Dietary Fiber 2g, Sugars 20g, Protein 5g*

Vegetarian

Whole Grain
Zucchini Bread

Preparation: 15 minutes | **Processing:** Pulsing plus 25 seconds
Bake Time: 1 hour 10 minutes | **Yield:** 1 loaf (12 slices)

1 ½ cups (300 g) granulated
sugar, divided use

2 ¼ teaspoons ground cinnamon,
divided use

2 ½ cups (312 g) all-purpose flour

1 cup (80 g) uncooked rolled oats

1 teaspoon baking powder

¾ teaspoon salt

½ teaspoon baking soda

10 ounces (284 g) zucchini,
cut into large chunks

3 large eggs

½ cup (122 g)
unsweetened applesauce

1 teaspoon vanilla extract

¼ cup (56 g) unsalted butter

1 cup (120 g) chopped walnuts
or pecans

¾ cup (120 g) raisins

Chef's Note

To chop nuts in your
Vitamix machine, place
them in the container and
secure the lid. Select
Variable 10. Pulse 10 to 20
times or until desired
chop is reached. For best
results, chop 2 cups at a
time, and store leftovers
at room temperature in an
airtight container.

1. Preheat oven to 350°F (180°C). Spray a 9-inch x 5-inch (23 cm x 13 cm)
   loaf pan with cooking spray.

2. Combine 1 Tablespoon sugar and ¼ teaspoon cinnamon and set aside.

3. Place flour, oats, baking powder, salt, baking soda, and 2 teaspoons cinnamon
   in a large-size mixing bowl and stir by hand to combine.

4. Place zucchini into the Vitamix container and secure lid.

5. Select Variable 4.

6. Pulse 3 times. Stop machine and remove lid. Scrape down the sides of the container
   with a spatula. Secure lid and Pulse 3 more times. Repeat this process once more.
   Place zucchini in a strainer to drain extra moisture.

7. Place eggs, remaining sugar, applesauce, vanilla and butter into the Vitamix container
   in the order listed and secure lid.

8. Select Variable 1.

Whole Grain Zucchini Bread continues on page 84

continued from page 83

Whole Grain Zucchini Bread

9. Switch machine to Start and slowly increase speed to Variable 5.

10. Blend for 15 seconds. Stop machine and remove lid. Scrape down the sides of the container with a spatula and secure lid. Reduce speed to Variable 2. Switch machine to Start and blend for 10 seconds.

11. Pour wet mixture into dry ingredients and stir by had to combine. Fold in chopped zucchini, nuts, and raisins. Spoon into prepared pan and sprinkle with cinnamon-sugar mixture.

12. Bake for 1 hour 10 minutes or until a toothpick inserted into the center comes out clean. Cool in pan on wire rack for 10 minutes. Remove from pan and cool completely on wire rack.

Nutritional Information

Amount Per Slice: *Calories 380, Total Fat 12g, Saturated Fat 3.5g, Cholesterol 55mg, Sodium 260mg, Total Carbohydrate 61g, Dietary Fiber 3g, Sugars 34g, Protein 7g*

Vegetarian

Multi-Seed Loaf

Preparation: 30 minutes | **Processing:** 15 seconds
Bake Time: 50–55 minutes | **Yield:** 1 loaf (12 slices)

1 ½ cups (188 g) all-purpose flour

½ cup (60 g) whole wheat flour

1 teaspoon baking powder

1 teaspoon baking soda

½ teaspoon salt

¾ cup (165 g) lightly packed
brown sugar

½ cup (60 g) shelled raw
sunflower seeds, lightly toasted

⅓ cup (35 g) flaxseed meal

2 Tablespoons (21 g)
whole flaxseed

2 Tablespoons (19 g)
poppy seeds

2 Tablespoons (17 g)
sesame seeds

1 large egg

1 ¼ cups (300 ml)
low-fat buttermilk

¼ cup (60 ml) vegetable oil

For garnish:

1 teaspoon whole flaxseed

1 teaspoon sesame seed

1 teaspoon shelled raw
sunflower seeds

Chef's Note

Toast sunflower seeds
*in a dry skillet over
medium-high heat until
lightly browned. Toss
pan frequently to
prevent burning.
Let cool 10 minutes.*

1. Preheat oven to 350°F (180°C). Spray a 9-inch x 5-inch (23 cm x 13 cm)
   loaf pan with cooking spray.

2. Place flours, baking powder, baking soda, salt, brown sugar, sunflower seeds, flaxseed
   meal, whole flaxseed, poppy seed, and sesame seed in a large-size mixing bowl.
   Stir by hand to combine.

3. Place egg, buttermilk and oil into the Vitamix container and secure lid.

4. Select Variable 2.

5. Switch machine to Start and blend for 15 seconds.

6. Pour wet mixture into dry ingredients and stir by hand to combine.

7. Pour batter into prepared loaf pan. Sprinkle with garnishes.

Multi-Seed Loaf continues on page 86

continued from page 85

Multi-Seed Loaf

8. Bake for 50 to 55 minutes or until a knife inserted into the center comes out clean.

9. Cool in pan for 10 minutes. Remove from pan and cool completely.

Nutritional Information

Amount Per Slice: *Calories 270, Total Fat 12g, Saturated Fat 1.5g, Cholesterol 15mg, Sodium 310mg, Total Carbohydrate 33g, Dietary Fiber 3g, Sugars 15g, Protein 7g*

Vegetarian

Cranberry Nut Bread

Preparation: 15 minutes | **Processing:** 15 seconds
Bake Time: 60 minutes | **Yield:** 1 loaf (10 slices)

1 cup (120 g) whole wheat flour

1 cup (125 g) all-purpose flour

1 ½ teaspoons baking powder

½ teaspoon baking soda

1 teaspoon salt

1 orange, peeled, with
2-inch (5 cm) strip of peel
remaining, and halved

¼ cup (60 ml) light olive
oil or vegetable oil

¾ cup (180 ml) skim milk

1 cup (200 g) granulated sugar

1 large egg

1 cup (100 g) fresh cranberries

½ cup (60 g) chopped walnuts

Chef's Note

Whether you're vegan or require a diet that's egg-free, you can still enjoy this homemade bread. Simply substitute the egg in this recipe for Ener-G Egg Replacer™ (or an egg substitute of your choice) and the soy milk for skim milk.

1. Preheat oven to 350°F (180°C). Spray an 8 ½-inch x 4 ½-inch (22 cm x 11 cm) loaf pan with cooking spray.

2. Combine flours, baking powder, baking soda, and salt in a large-size mixing bowl. Set aside.

3. Place orange, oil, milk, sugar, and egg into the Vitamix container in the order listed and secure lid.

4. Select Variable 1.

5. Switch machine to Start and slowly increase speed to Variable 10.

6. Blend for 15 seconds.

7. Pour orange juice mixture into dry ingredients, stirring by hand until ingredients are just moistened.

8. Gently stir in cranberries and chopped walnuts. Spread batter in prepared loaf pan.

9. Bake for 60 minutes or until a knife inserted into the center comes out clean.

Nutritional Information

Amount Per Slice: *Calories 280, Total Fat 10g, Saturated Fat 1.5g, Cholesterol 20mg, Sodium 380mg, Total Carbohydrate 43g, Dietary Fiber 3g, Sugars 23g, Protein 5g*

Vegetarian

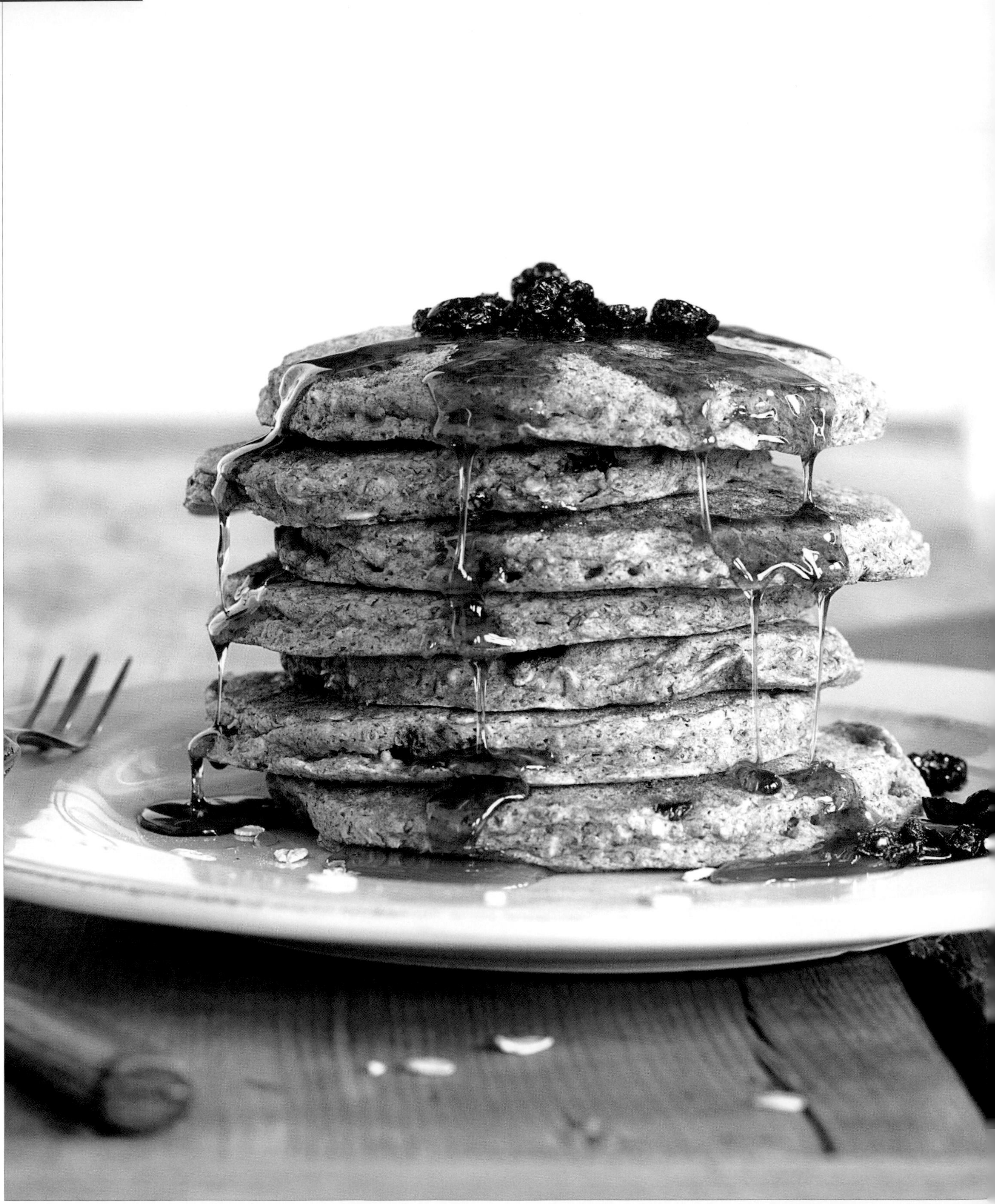

Oatmeal Cranberry Pancakes

Preparation: 15 minutes plus rest time | ***Processing:*** 20 seconds | ***Yield:*** 12 pancakes

1 ½ cups (360 ml) unsweetened almond or soy milk

1 ½ teaspoons Ener-G egg replacer

2 Tablespoons (30 ml) water

1 cup (120 g) whole wheat flour

2 teaspoons baking powder

½ teaspoon baking soda

¼ cup (40 g) flaxseed meal

¾ cup (115 g) uncooked rolled oats

¼ cup (30 g) dried cranberries

2 Tablespoons (20 g) unsalted sunflower seeds

1. Place almond milk, egg replacer, water, flour, baking powder, baking soda, and flaxseed meal into the Vitamix container in the order listed and secure lid.

2. Select Variable 1.

3. Switch machine to Start and slowly increase speed to Variable 10.

4. Blend for 10 seconds. Stop machine and remove lid.

5. Add oats, cranberries, and sunflower seeds into the Vitamix container and secure lid.

6. Select Variable 2.

7. Switch machine to Start and blend for 10 seconds, using the tamper to press the ingredients into the blades.

8. Let batter sit for 5 to 10 minutes before cooking to yield best texture and flavor.

Nutritional Information

Amount Per Pancake: *Calories 80, Total Fat 2.5g, Saturated Fat 0g, Cholesterol 0mg, Sodium 160mg, Total Carbohydrate 14g, Dietary Fiber 3g, Sugars 2g, Protein 3g*

Vegan

Vegetarian

Dairy-free

Peanut Butter and Banana Muffins

Preparation: 20 minutes | ***Processing:*** 15 seconds | ***Bake Time:*** 20 minutes | ***Yield:*** 24 muffins

3 cups (375 g) all-purpose flour

1 Tablespoon baking powder

¼ teaspoon salt

¾ cup (180 ml) 2% milk

2 large eggs

1 Tablespoon vanilla extract

2 ripe medium bananas, peeled

¾ cup (192 g) peanut butter

⅓ cup (75 g) unsalted butter, softened

1 ½ cups (300 g) granulated sugar

⅓ cup (27 g) uncooked rolled oats

1. Preheat oven to 400°F (200°C). Line two 12-cup muffin tins with paper liners.

2. Place flour, baking powder, and salt in a large-size mixing bowl and stir by hand to combine.

3. Place milk, eggs, vanilla, bananas, peanut butter, butter, and sugar into the Vitamix container in the order listed and secure lid.

4. Select Variable 5.

5. Switch machine to Start and blend for 15 seconds.

6. Pour wet mixture into dry ingredients and stir by hand to combine.

7. Spoon into lined muffin cups. Sprinkle oats over batter. Bake 20 minute or until a toothpick inserted into the center comes out clean. Cool on wire racks.

Nutritional Information

Amount Per Muffin: *Calories 150, Total Fat 2.5g, Saturated Fat 0.5g, Cholesterol 15mg, Sodium 110mg, Total Carbohydrate 29g, Dietary Fiber 1g, Sugars 15g, Protein 4g*

Vegetarian

Lemon Ginger Muffins

Preparation: 15 minutes | **Processing:** 30 seconds
Bake Time: 15–20 minutes | **Yield:** 12 muffins

2 cups (250 g) plus
2 teaspoons all-purpose flour,
divided use

1 Tablespoon freshly grated
lemon zest plus 2 teaspoons,
divided use

1 ¾ teaspoons baking powder

¼ teaspoon salt

¾ cup (150 g) granulated
sugar, divided use

¼ cup (60 g) crystallized
ginger, small pieces

⅓ cup (75 g) unsalted butter,
softened plus 3 Tablespoons
(42 g), divided use

1 large egg

¾ cup (180 ml) milk

1 Tablespoon fresh lemon juice

1. Preheat oven to 350°F (180°C). Spray a 12-cup muffin tin with cooking spray or line with paper liners; set aside.

2. In a medium-size mixing bowl, mix together flour, 1 Tablespoon lemon zest, baking powder, and salt; set aside.

3. Place ½ cup (100 g) sugar and crystallized ginger into the Vitamix container and secure lid.

4. Select Variable 1.

5. Switch machine to Start and slowly increase speed to Variable 5.

6. Blend for 5 seconds. Stop machine and remove lid.

7. Add ⅓ cup (75 g) butter to the Vitamix container and secure lid.

8. Select Variable 1.

9. Switch machine to Start and slowly increase speed to Variable 6.

10. Blend for 10 seconds. Stop machine and remove lid. Scrape down the sides of the container with a spatula.

11. Add egg and milk to the Vitamix container and secure lid.

Lemon Ginger Muffins continues on page 92

Reinvent the Breakfast Basket

A tasty gift basket is sure to brighten anyone's morning — especially if the goodies come straight from your kitchen. Fill mason jars with homemade Cinnamon Nut Butter or Chocolate Hazelnut Spread (See Breakfast Condiments) to accompany an assortment of muffins and breads.

Add a sampling of seasonings to sprinkle on a morning coffee cup. Go gourmet with maple flakes, ground vanilla, or granulated honey. Your thoughtfulness will be appreciated long after their morning coffee break.

continued from page 91

Lemon Ginger Muffins

12. Select Variable 1.

13. Switch machine to Start and slowly increase speed to Variable 6.

14. Blend for 15 seconds.

15. Pour wet mixture into dry ingredients and stir by hand until well-combined.

16. Spoon ¼ cup (60 g) batter into each muffin tin.

17. Bake until toothpick inserted into the center comes out clean and edges are very lightly browned (15 to 20 minutes).

18. Meanwhile, in a small bowl, stir together ¼ cup (50 g) sugar and 2 teaspoons lemon zest; set aside.

19. In another small bowl, stir together 3 Tablespoons (45 ml) melted butter and lemon juice; set aside.

20. When muffins are finished baking and still hot, roll tops in melted butter mixture, then in sugar and lemon zest mixture.

21. Place muffins on wire rack to cool.

Nutritional Information

Amount Per Muffin: *Calories 230, Total Fat 9g, Saturated Fat 6g, Cholesterol 40mg, Sodium 135mg, Total Carbohydrate 34g, Dietary Fiber 1g, Sugars 15g, Protein 3g*

Vegetarian

Whole Wheat Crêpes

Preparation: 45 minutes | **Processing:** 15 seconds
Cook Time: 10 minutes | **Yield:** 14 crêpes

1 cup (120 g) whole wheat flour

1 cup (125 g) all-purpose flour

½ teaspoon salt

1 cup (240 ml) 2% milk

6 large eggs

4 teaspoons canola oil

2 teaspoons granulated sugar

1 cup (240 ml) seltzer water

1. Place flours and salt in a medium-size mixing bowl and stir by hand to combine.

2. Place milk, eggs, oil, and sugar into the Vitamix container in the order listed and secure lid.

3. Select Variable 1.

4. Switch machine to Start and slowly increase speed to Variable 5.

5. Blend for 15 seconds.

6. Pour wet mixture into dry ingredients and use a whisk to combine.
Cover and refrigerate at least 30 minutes.

7. Slowly whisk seltzer water into the batter.

8. Spray a nonstick skillet with cooking spray, heat over medium-high. Ladle ⅓ cup (80 ml) batter onto the center of the pan and immediately tilt and rotate the pan to spread the batter evenly over the bottom.

9. Cook about 30 seconds, until underside is lightly browned. Use a heat-resistant spatula to lift the edge of the crêpe and then grab with your fingers to flip. Cook until second side is lightly browned. Slide onto plate. Repeat with remaining batter. Cover crêpes with waxed paper as you prepare the filling.

Nutritional Information

Amount Per Crêpe: *Calories 120, Total Fat 4g, Saturated Fat 1g, Cholesterol 80mg, Sodium 120mg, Total Carbohydrate 15g, Dietary Fiber 1g, Sugars 2g, Protein 5g*

Vegetarian

Garden Fresh Crêpe Filling

Preparation: 15 minutes | ***Processing:*** Pulsing | ***Cook Time:*** 10 minutes | ***Yield:*** 6 crêpes

3 cups (290 g) whole
button mushrooms

4 ounces (114 g) shallots

5 ounces (140 g) baby spinach

1 Tablespoon olive oil

1 teaspoon chopped
fresh rosemary

½ teaspoon salt

6 Tablespoons (102 g) goat cheese

6 Whole Wheat Crêpes (page 93)

1. Place mushrooms and shallots into the Vitamix container and secure lid.

2. Select Variable 4.

3. Pulse 5 times. Remove lid and scrape down the sides of the container with a spatula. Secure lid
   and Pulse 5 more times. Repeat this process until all of the mushrooms are chopped. Empty into a bowl.

4. Place spinach into the Vitamix container and secure lid.

5. Select Variable 4.

6. Pulse 5 times using the tamper. Remove lid and scrape down the sides of the container with a spatula.
   Secure lid and Pulse 5 more times. Repeat this process until all of the spinach is chopped.

7. Heat olive oil in a large nonstick skillet over medium heat. Add mushrooms, shallot, rosemary and salt.
   Cook, stirring until the mushrooms are soft, about 5 minutes. Stir in chopped spinach a handful at a
   time; cook until wilted, about 4 minutes.

8. Place crêpe on a clean cutting board or plate. Spread filling in the center, leaving a 1 to 2-inch (2.5 cm – 5 cm)
   border. Top with a Tablespoon of goat cheese. Fold approximately two inches of each side of the crêpe
   toward the center. Garnish with fresh chopped rosemary. Repeat with 5 remaining crêpes.

Nutritional Information

Amount Per Crêpe: *Calories 210, Total Fat 10g, Saturated Fat 4g, Cholesterol 90mg,
Sodium 420mg, Total Carbohydrate 22g, Dietary Fiber 2g, Sugars 4g, Protein 10g*

Vegetarian

Apple Pancakes

Preparation: 15 minutes | **Processing:** 20 seconds | **Yield:** 26 pancakes (13 servings)

2 cups (240 g) whole wheat flour

2 Tablespoons (30 g)
baking powder

1 teaspoon baking soda

1 teaspoon salt

6 Tablespoons (75 g)
granulated sugar

½ teaspoon ground nutmeg

2 cups (480 ml) milk

2 large eggs

1 Tablespoon butter

½ teaspoon vanilla extract

1 medium apple, 5 ounces (142 g),
cored and quartered

1. Add flour, baking powder, baking soda, salt, sugar, and nutmeg to a
   medium-size mixing bowl. Stir by hand to combine. Set aside.

2. Place milk, eggs, butter, vanilla, and apple into the Vitamix container
   in the order listed and secure lid.

3. Select Variable 1.

4. Switch machine to Start and slowly increase speed to Variable 5.

5. Blend for 20 seconds.

6. Pour wet mixture into dry ingredients and stir by hand to combine.

7. Let batter sit for 5 to 10 minutes before cooking to yield best texture and flavor.

Nutritional Information

Amount Per 2 Pancake Serving: *Calories 130, Total Fat 3.5g, Saturated Fat 1.5g, Cholesterol 35mg, Sodium 540mg, Total Carbohydrate 23g, Dietary Fiber 2g, Sugars 9g, Protein 5g*

Vegetarian

Holiday Hot Cakes with Sweet Raspberry Topping

Preparation: 20 minutes | ***Processing:*** 1 minute | ***Cook Time:*** 15–20 minutes
Yield: 2 ⅓ cups (560 ml) syrup, 16 pancakes

4 cups (454 g) frozen unsweetened raspberries, divided use

½ cup (120 ml) water

½ cup (120 ml) honey plus
⅓ cup (80 ml), divided use

2 cups (240 g) whole wheat flour

1 ½ teaspoons baking powder

½ teaspoon baking soda

½ teaspoon ground cinnamon

½ teaspoon ground ginger

4 ½ teaspoons Ener-G egg replacer

6 Tablespoons (90 ml) water

1 ½ cups (360 ml) unsweetened almond or soy milk

1 cup (240 g) canned pumpkin purée

½ teaspoon vanilla extract

1. Place 3 cups (340 g) raspberries and water in a saucepan. Bring to a boil, cover, and cook 5 minutes. Let cool 10 minutes.

2. Place mixture into the Vitamix container, add ½ cup (120 ml) honey, and secure lid.

3. Select Variable 1.

4. Switch machine to Start and slowly increase speed to Variable 10.

5. Blend for 45 seconds. Return to saucepan and add remaining berries. Keep warm until serving.

6. Combine flour, baking powder, baking soda, cinnamon, and ginger by hand in a large-size mixing bowl.

7. Place egg replacer, water, ⅓ cup (80 ml) honey, almond milk, pumpkin, and vanilla into the Vitamix container in the order listed and secure lid.

8. Select Variable 1.

Holiday Hot Cakes with Sweet Raspberry Topping *continues on page 98*

continued from page 97

Holiday Hot Cakes with Sweet Raspberry Topping

9. Switch machine to Start and slowly increase speed to Variable 4. Blend for 15 seconds.

10. Pour wet mixture into dry ingredients and fold by hand to combine.

11. Heat a nonstick griddle over medium-high heat. Ladle ⅓ cup (80 ml) onto skillet for each pancake. Cook 2 minutes each side.

12. Serve with raspberry topping and dust with powdered sugar.

Nutritional Information

Amount Per 4 Pancakes with ¼ Cup (60 g) Topping: *Calories 400, Total Fat 3g, Saturated Fat 0g, Cholesterol 0mg, Sodium 420mg, Total Carbohydrate 91g, Dietary Fiber 10g, Sugars 36g, Protein 10g*

Vegetarian   Dairy-free

Carrot Raisin Muffins

Preparation: 20 minutes | **Processing:** 20 seconds
Bake Time: 20–25 minutes | **Yield:** 12 muffins

1 ⅔ cups (200 g) self-rising flour

½ teaspoon baking soda

1 teaspoon ground cinnamon

1 teaspoon pumpkin pie spice

1 cup (165 g) raisins

⅔ cup (160 ml) light olive oil

2 large eggs

¾ cup (150 g) granulated sugar

¾ cup (100 g) chopped carrots

Chef's Note

On the weekends, bake a batch of muffins and wrap them individually for freezing. In the morning, pop one in the microwave for a few seconds and you've got a warm, tasty breakfast to go.

1. Preheat oven to 350°F (180°C). Spray a 12-cup muffin tin with cooking spray or line with paper liners.

2. Place flour, baking soda, cinnamon, and pumpkin pie spice in a medium-size mixing bowl and stir lightly. Stir in raisins. Set aside.

3. Place oil, eggs, sugar, and carrots into the Vitamix container and secure lid.

4. Select Variable 1.

5. Switch machine to Start and slowly increase speed to Variable 6.

6. Blend for 20 seconds until thick and creamy.

7. Pour carrot mixture into flour mixture and fold by hand to combine. Spoon the mixture into prepared muffin tin.

8. Bake for 20 to 25 minutes until golden-brown. Transfer to a wire rack to cool before serving.

Nutritional Information

Amount Per Muffin: *Calories 270, Total Fat 13g, Saturated Fat 2g, Cholesterol 30mg, Sodium 300mg, Total Carbohydrate 37g, Dietary Fiber 1g, Sugars 23g, Protein 3g*

Vegetarian   **Dairy-free**

Coconut Waffles

Preparation: 20 minutes | **Processing:** 10 seconds
Yield: 7 waffles

1 ¾ cups (220 g) all-purpose flour

2 Tablespoons (25 g)
granulated sugar

1 Tablespoon baking powder

3 large eggs

1 (14-ounce/400 ml)
can light coconut milk

6 Tablespoons (85 g)
butter, softened

¾ cup (60 g) unsweetened
shredded coconut

½ cup (72 g) almonds,
chopped and toasted

Chef's Note

Toast almonds in a dry
skillet over medium-high
heat until deeply
browned. Toss pan
frequently to prevent
burning. Let cool 10
minutes. Place almonds
into the Vitamix container
and secure lid. Select
Variable 5. Pulse 5 times
or until chopped.

1. Place flour, sugar, and baking powder in a medium-size mixing bowl and stir by hand to combine.

2. Place eggs, coconut milk, butter, and coconut into the Vitamix container in the order listed and secure lid.

3. Select Variable 5.

4. Switch machine to Start and blend for 10 seconds.

5. Pour wet mixture into dry ingredients and stir by hand to combine.

6. Place ½ cup (120 ml) batter onto a preheated waffle maker. Bake according to manufacturer's instructions.

7. Garnish with toasted almonds.

Nutritional Information

Amount Per Waffle: Calories 390, Total Fat 26g, Saturated Fat 15g, Cholesterol 105mg, Sodium 340mg, Total Carbohydrate 33g, Dietary Fiber 3g, Sugars 5g, Protein 9g

Vegetarian

Oven Baked Onion Cheese Frittata

Preparation: 20 minutes | **Processing:** 15 seconds
Bake Time: 20–25 minutes | **Yield:** 8 servings

¼ cup (40 g) chopped onion

1 cup (115 g) diced
summer squash

¼ cup (40 g) diced red
bell pepper

¼ cup (40 g) diced green
bell pepper

2 Tablespoons (30 ml) olive oil

6 large eggs

½ cup (50 g) grated
Parmesan cheese

½ teaspoon dried oregano

⅛ teaspoon ground nutmeg

½ teaspoon salt

¼ teaspoon ground black pepper

½ cup (65 g) Cheddar
cheese, cubed

1. Preheat oven to 350°F (180°C). Spray a 9-inch (23 cm) pie pan with cooking spray.

2. Sauté onion, squash, and peppers in olive oil until soft. Place in bottom of prepared pie pan.

3. Place eggs, Parmesan, oregano, nutmeg, salt, and pepper into the Vitamix container in the order listed and secure lid. Select Variable 1.

4. Switch machine to Start and slowly increase speed to Variable 4.

5. Blend for 10 seconds.

6. Remove lid plug. Add Cheddar cheese through the lid plug opening and blend an additional 5 seconds.

7. Pour mixture over vegetables. Bake 20 to 25 minutes or until set.

Nutritional Information

Amount Per Serving: *Calories 150, Total Fat 11g, Saturated Fat 4.5g, Cholesterol 150mg, Sodium 330mg, Total Carbohydrate 2g, Dietary Fiber 0g, Sugars 1 g, Protein 9g*

Vegetarian **Gluten-free**

On the Menu

Brunch Buffet

A buffet can be a real lifesaver when entertaining a large group. For simpler self-serving and lovely presentation, create individual frittatas for your guests.

Place about a tablespoon of the vegetable mixture in each cup of a paper-lined muffin tin, then fill with blended egg mixture. Individual frittatas also make delicious hors d'oeuvres for a baby or bridal shower. With all the different paper muffin cups available, you can coordinate them to match the colors of the event for an extra special touch.

Chef's Note

If you prefer *an egg alternative such as Egg Beaters, substitute ¼ cup for every egg included in the recipe.*

Quiche with Brown Rice Crust

Preparation: 1 hour | **Processing:** 20 seconds
Bake Time: 50 – 55 minutes | **Yield:** 8 servings

Brown Rice Crust:

2 cups (390 g) cooked
brown rice, cooled

1 large egg white

Quiche Filling:

1 cup (70 g) chopped
broccoli florets, steamed

3 large eggs

¾ cup (180 ml) milk

½ cup (55 g) shredded
Cheddar cheese

1 Tablespoon fresh parsley

1 ½ Tablespoons dried basil

¼ teaspoon salt

¼ teaspoon onion powder

1. Preheat oven to 350°F (180°C). Spray a 9-inch (23 cm) pie pan with cooking spray. Mix rice and egg white in a medium-size bowl by hand. Press into prepared pan and bake for 10 minutes.

2. Preheat oven to 400°F (200°C).

3. Place broccoli in center of baked rice crust.

4. Add eggs milk, cheese, parsley, basil, salt, and onion powder into the Vitamix container in the order listed and secure lid. Select Variable 1.

5. Switch machine to Start and slowly increase speed to Variable 3.

6. Blend for 20 seconds.

7. Pour mixture over broccoli and bake 40 to 45 minutes or until top is brown.

Nutritional Information

Amount Per Serving: *Calories 130, Total Fat 5g, Saturated Fat 2.5g, Cholesterol 80mg, Sodium 160mg, Total Carbohydrate 14g, Dietary Fiber 1g, Sugars 1g, Protein 7g*

Vegetarian **Gluten-free**

Potato Cheddar Breakfast Bake

Preparation: 20 minutes | **Processing:** 20–25 seconds
Bake Time: 1 hour 20 minutes | **Yield:** 10 servings

1 ¼ pounds (568 g)
Russet potatoes, cubed

8 large eggs

2 cups (480 ml) milk

½ teaspoon salt

8 ounces (227 g) Cheddar
cheese, cut into large cubes

¼ cup (40 g) chopped
green pepper

¼ cup (40 g) chopped onion

1 ½ cups (210 g) diced ham

1. Preheat oven to 350°F (180°C). Spray a 9-inch x 9-inch (23 cm x 23 cm) baking pan with cooking spray.

2. Hash potatoes using the wet chop method. Drain well and reserve.

3. Place eggs, milk, salt, and cheese into the Vitamix container in the order listed and secure lid. Select Variable 1.

4. Switch machine to Start and slowly increase speed to Variable 5.

5. Blend for 10 seconds. Reduce speed to Variable 2 and remove lid plug.

6. Add peppers, onion, potatoes, and ham through the lid plug opening.

7. Blend for 10 to 15 seconds.

8. Pour into prepared pan. Bake covered for 40 to 45 minutes. Uncover and bake an additional 30 to 35 minutes until firm and lightly browned.

Nutritional Information

Amount Per Serving: *Calories 270, Total Fat 15g, Saturated Fat 8g, Cholesterol 195mg, Sodium 350mg, Total Carbohydrate 14g, Dietary Fiber 1g, Sugars 3g, Protein 19g*

Gluten-free

What Is Wet Chopping?

When you need a uniform cut, like hashing potatoes for this breakfast bake or prepping cabbage for slaw, use the wet chop method. In this Vitamix technique, water draws ingredients into the blades, resulting in a uniform chop. The type of chop, whether coarse or fine, is determined by the speed selected on the Variable Speed Dial.

Fill the Vitamix container with quartered potatoes to the 4-cup level. Add water to the 6-cup level and secure lid. Select Variable 5 and pulse 4 to 5 times until chopped. Drain well. Spread potatoes out on a cookie sheet and press with paper towels to absorb any excess liquid.

Homemade Peanut Butter

Preparation: 5 minutes | *Processing:* 1 minute 30 seconds | *Yield:* 2 cups (480 ml) (16 servings)

4 cups (590 g) unsalted
dry roasted peanuts

1. Place nuts into the Vitamix container and secure lid.

2. Select Variable 1.

3. Switch machine to Start and slowly increase speed to Variable 10.

4. Use the tamper to press the ingredients into the blades.

5. In about 1 minute, you will hear a high-pitched chugging sound.

6. Blend for an additional 30 seconds or until desired consistency is reached.

7. Store refrigerated in an airtight container for up to 1 week.
   It can also be frozen for longer storage.

Nutritional Information

Amount Per 2 Tablespoon (30 g) Serving: Calories 210, Total Fat 18g, Saturated Fat 2.5g, Cholesterol 0mg, Sodium 0mg, Total Carbohydrate 8g, Dietary Fiber 3g, Sugars 2g, Protein 9g

Vegan   **Vegetarian**   **Dairy-free**   **Gluten-free**

Cinnamon Nut Butter

Preparation: 10 minutes | **Processing:** 1 minute
Yield: 2 ¼ cups (540 ml) (18 servings)

2 cups (280 g) unsalted dry roasted peanuts

1 cup (145 g) blanched almonds

¼ teaspoon ground cinnamon

1 cup (120 g) unsalted pecan halves or pieces

1. Place all ingredients into the Vitamix container in the order listed and secure lid.

2. Select Variable 1.

3. Switch machine to Start and slowly increase speed to Variable 10.

4. Blend for about 1 minute, using the tamper to press the ingredients into the blades.

Nutritional Information

Amount Per 2 Tablespoon (30 ml) Serving: Calories 190, Total Fat 17g, Saturated Fat 2g, Cholesterol 0mg, Sodium 0mg, Total Carbohydrate 6g, Dietary Fiber 3g, Sugars 1g, Protein 6g

Vegan   **Vegetarian**   **Dairy-free**   **Gluten-free**

Chef's Note

Try experimenting with other natural sweeteners for unique flavored butters. Honey and maple syrup pair well with warm breakfast breads. For greater variety, substitute the peanuts, almonds, or pecans for different nuts such as cashews or walnuts.

Fresh Applesauce

Preparation: 10 minutes | ***Processing:*** 20–25 seconds
Yield: 2 cups (480 ml) (4 servings)

4 medium apples, 1 ½ pounds
(680 g), cored and quartered

2 Tablespoons (30 ml) fresh
lemon juice

1. Place all ingredients into the Vitamix container in the order
   listed and secure lid.

2. Select Variable 1.

3. Switch machine to Start and slowly increase speed to Variable 5.

4. Blend for 20 to 25 seconds or until desired consistency is reached.

Nutritional Information

Amount Per Serving: *Calories 110, Total Fat 0g, Saturated Fat 0g,
Cholesterol 0mg, Sodium 0mg, Total Carbohydrate 30g, Dietary Fiber 5g,
Sugars 2g, Protein 1g*

Vegan   **Vegetarian**   **Raw**   **Dairy-free**   **Gluten-free**

Ingredient IQ

Apple Varieties

Certain apple varieties lend
themselves best to baking,
while others make better
sauces and snacks, but it's
really a matter of personal
preference in regards to flavor.
Some people prefer apple
varieties that are mildly tart
and crisp versus apples that
are sweet and juicy.

Apple varieties such as
Cortland, Empire, Macoun,
and McIntosh are great for
saucing because of how well
they break down with heat.
Some of the best apples
for baking whole are Rome,
Granny Smith, Braeburn,
Golden Delicious, and
Jonagold, as they maintain
their shape well when cooking.

Honeycrisp and Fuji apples
are two of the sweetest
apple varieties, making them
perfect for eating raw or
adding to salads.

Chef's Note

For a low-sugar version of your favorite jams and jellies, make sure to purchase low methoxyl pectin.

Fruit Jelly

Preparation: 10 minutes | **Processing:** 30 seconds
Cook Time: 30 minutes | **Yield:** 6 cups (1.4 l) (96 servings)

2 cups (480 g) fresh or frozen unsweetened fruit,
cut into large pieces

3 cups (720 ml) water

1 (1.75-ounce/50 g) package fruit pectin

4 ½ cups (900 g) granulated sugar

1. Place fruit and water into the Vitamix container and secure lid.

2. Select Variable 1.

3. Switch machine to Start and slowly increase speed to Variable 10.

4. Blend for 30 seconds or until smooth.

5. Pour contents into a 4-cup (960 ml) capacity measuring cup.
   Add additional water to equal 4 cups (960 ml) if necessary.

6. Transfer to a Dutch oven or similar size pot. Stir in fruit pectin.

7. Place pot over high heat, stirring constantly until mixture comes to a hard boil.

8. Add sugar and bring to a full rolling boil for 1 minute.

9. If canning, follow standard canning procedure. If storing in a refrigerator, place in
   airtight container. Product may be refrigerated for up to 4 weeks.

Nutritional Information

Amount per 1 Tablespoon serving: *Calories 40, Total Fat 0g, Saturated Fat 0g, Cholesterol 0mg, Sodium 0mg, Total Carbohydrate 10g, Dietary Fiber 0g, Sugars 10g, Protein 0g*

Vegan

Vegetarian

Dairy-free

Gluten-free

Chocolate Hazelnut Spread

Preparation: 10 minutes | ***Processing:*** 5–6 minutes
Bake Time: 15 minutes | ***Yield:*** 1 ½ cups (360 ml) (12 servings)

1 cup (200 g) granulated sugar

½ cup (120 ml) water

4 cups (540 g) raw hazelnuts

½ cup (43 g) unsweetened cocoa powder

1 ½ teaspoons vanilla extract

2 Tablespoons (30 ml) light olive oil

⅛ teaspoon salt

1. Preheat oven to 350°F (180°C). Line a baking sheet with foil.

2. Combine sugar and water in a 3 to 4 cup saucepan. Cover and bring the mixture to a simmer over medium heat. Remove the lid and wipe down the sides of the pan with a wet pastry brush or a scrunched-up paper towel dipped in water. Cover and cook for 2 minutes or until the sugar is completely dissolved. Uncover and cook until the syrup looks like pale amber maple syrup.

3. Immediately pour the caramel onto the lined baking sheet. Tilt the sheet to spread the caramel as thinly as possible. Let harden completely, about 15 minutes.

4. Place hazelnuts in a single layer on a baking sheet. Toast in the oven until the skins are almost black and the meat is dark brown, about 15 minutes. Stir the nuts halfway through baking to ensure an even color.

5. To remove skins, wrap cooled hazelnuts in a clean kitchen towel. Rub until most of the skins come off.

6. Break cooled caramel into small pieces, place them into the Vitamix container, and secure lid.

7. Select Variable 1.

8. Switch machine to Start and slowly increase speed to Variable 10.

9. Blend for 15 seconds. Stop machine and remove lid.

10. Add the nuts to the Vitamix container and secure lid.

Chocolate Hazelnut Spread *continues on page 114*

Make It Your Own

Spread the News

Chocolate Hazelnut Spread is a delicious alternative to butter or jam on toast and croissants and makes a wonderful filling for pastries and desserts.

Delight guests with a breakfast menu of Whole Wheat Crêpes (See Breakfasts) filled with Chocolate Hazelnut Spread and bananas, accompanied by Cranberry Nut Bread (See Breakfasts), fresh strawberries, and a steaming mug of Cappuccino (See Beverages).

continued from page 113

Chocolate Hazelnut Spread

11. Select Variable 1.

12. Switch machine to Start and slowly increase speed to Variable 10.

13. Blend for 1 minute, using the tamper to press the ingredients into the blades.
Stop machine and remove lid. Scrape down the sides of the container with a spatula
and secure lid. Continue blending until nuts liquefy.

14. Add remaining ingredients to the Vitamix container and secure lid.

15. Select Variable 1.

16. Switch machine to Start and slowly increase speed to Variable 8.

17. Blend for 4 minutes, using the tamper to press the ingredients into the blades.

Nutritional Information

Amount Per 2 Tablespoon (30 ml) Serving: *Calories 380, Total Fat 30g, Saturated Fat 2.5g,
Cholesterol 0mg, Sodium 25mg, Total Carbohydrate 26g, Dietary Fiber 6g, Sugars 19g, Protein 7g*

Vegan   **Vegetarian**   **Dairy-free**   **Gluten-free**

Blueberry Syrup

Preparation: 10 minutes | *Processing:* 3 – 4 minutes
Yield: 2 cups (480 ml) (8 servings)

3 cups (454 g) fresh or frozen unsweetened,
thawed blueberries

½ cup (100 g) granulated sugar

1 teaspoon fresh lemon juice

1. Place all ingredients into the Vitamix container in the order
   listed and secure lid.

2. Select Variable 1.

3. Switch machine to Start and slowly increase speed to Variable 10.

4. Blend for 3 to 4 minutes.

5. For a traditional thicker syrup, place mixture in a pot
   and cook on medium heat for 30 minutes.

Nutritional Information

Amount Per ¼ Cup (60 ml) Serving: *Calories 80, Total Fat 0g,
Saturated Fat 0g, Cholesterol 0mg, Sodium 0mg, Total Carbohydrate 21g,
Dietary Fiber 1g, Sugars 18g, Protein 0g*

Vegan   **Vegetarian**   **Dairy-free**   **Gluten-free**

Bright Idea

Sweet Syrups

Use this recipe as inspiration
for creating different flavored
fruit syrups. Try berries such
as strawberries, raspberries,
or blackberries and experiment
with flavor combinations until
you find your favorite.

In addition to topping waffles,
pancakes, and desserts,
fresh fruit syrups make great
beverage stir-ins. Just mix
1 ounce (30 ml) syrup with
8 to 12 ounces (240 to 360 ml)
club soda. Pour the mixture
over ice for a chilled and
refreshing beverage.

Soups

Vegan

Vegetarian

Dairy-free

Gluten-free

Soups are a healthy and easy meal for lunch or dinner. Transform fresh vegetables into rustic chilled soups like Gazpacho or steamy purées like Creamy Tomato and Basic Sweet Potato.

Soups

BISQUE / CHILI / CHOWDER / SOUPS

Chicken Potato Spinach Soup

Preparation: 15 minutes | **Processing:** 5 minutes 45 seconds
Yield: 5 ¼ cups (1.2 l) (5 servings)

1 cup (240 ml) Homemade Chicken Stock (page 163)

1 ½ cups (360 ml) unsweetened soy or almond milk

¼ cup (40 g) chopped onion

3 medium Russet potatoes (640 g), baked and halved, divided use

⅛ teaspoon dried rosemary

1 Tablespoon spinach, cooked or frozen, thawed

5 ounces (140 g) skinless, boneless chicken breast, cooked and diced

Sea salt, to taste

1. Place broth, milk, onion, two potatoes, and rosemary into the Vitamix container in the order listed and secure lid.

2. Select Variable 1.

3. Switch machine to Start and slowly increase speed to Variable 10.

4. Blend for 5 minutes 30 seconds.

5. Reduce speed to Variable 1 and remove lid plug.

6. Add spinach, remaining potato, and chicken through the lid plug opening. Replace lid plug and blend an additional 10 to 15 seconds.

7. Season to taste with sea salt, if desired.

Nutritional Information

Amount Per Serving: *Calories 190, Total Fat 7g, Saturated Fat 1.5g, Cholesterol 15mg, Sodium 135mg, Total Carbohydrate 22g, Dietary Fiber 2g, Sugars 2g, Protein 10g*

Dairy-free

Gluten-free

Vegetable Soup

Preparation: 30 minutes | **Processing:** 30-40 seconds | **Cook Time:** 30 minutes
Yield: 12 ½ cups (3.0 l) (12 servings)

⅓ cup (80 ml) extra virgin olive oil

5 garlic cloves, peeled and halved

3 medium carrots, 9 ounces
(256 g), rough chopped

2 stalks celery, 5 ounces (142 g),
rough chopped

1 medium yellow onion, 3 ½ ounces
(99 g), rough chopped

½ medium zucchini, 4 ½ ounces
(128 g), rough chopped

¼ head Savoy cabbage, 7 ½ ounces
(200 g), rough chopped

8 cups (1.9 l) Homemade
Vegetable Stock (page 162)

7 whole tomatoes, peeled,
or 1 (14–ounce/397 g) can
diced tomatoes

1 (15-ounce/425 g) can cannellini
beans, drained, divided use

½ pound (227 g) thin
spaghetti, cooked

Sea salt, to taste

1. Heat oil in a large saucepan over medium-high heat. Add garlic, carrots, celery, and onions. Cook covered, stirring occasionally until crisp-tender, 12 to 15 minutes.

2. Add zucchini and cabbage. Cook covered until wilted, 3 to 5 minutes.

3. Add broth and tomatoes. Bring to a boil and cook 5 minutes.

4. Carefully place half of the soup and half of the beans into the Vitamix container and secure lid. Select Variable 1.

5. Switch machine to Start and slowly increase speed to Variable 10.

6. Blend for 30 to 40 seconds. Return mixture to pot and add remaining beans. (Only half the soup mixture is blended to maintain a rustic texture.)

7. Serve over cooked spaghetti. Season to taste with sea salt, if desired.

Nutritional Information

Amount Per Serving: *Calories 180, Total Fat 7g, Saturated Fat 1g, Cholesterol 0mg, Sodium 170mg, Total Carbohydrate 26g, Dietary Fiber 4g, Sugars 5g, Protein 6g*

Vegan **Vegetarian** **Dairy-free** **Gluten-free**

Velvety Fennel Soup

Preparation: 20 minutes | ***Processing:*** Pulsing plus 30 seconds | ***Cook Time:*** 30–35 minutes
Yield: 3 ½ cups (840 ml) (3 servings)

2 Tablespoons (30 ml) extra virgin olive oil, divided use

2 cups (174 g) chopped fennel bulb, chop and reserve fronds

1 cup (124 g) diced zucchini

1 cup (160 g) chopped onion

¼ teaspoon fennel seeds

2 cups (480 ml) Homemade Chicken Stock (page 163)

¾ cup (112 g) grape tomatoes

Sea salt, to taste

Ground black pepper, to taste

1. Heat 1 Tablespoon oil in a large saucepan over medium heat. Add fennel bulb, zucchini, onion, and fennel seeds. Sauté until fennel is translucent, 5 to 6 minutes.

2. Add broth and bring to a boil. Cover, reduce heat and simmer until vegetables are tender, about 15 minutes. Transfer to a soup pot to keep warm.

3. For tomato garnish, place tomatoes into the Vitamix container and secure lid.

4. Select Variable 5.

5. Pulse 2 to 3 times to chop tomatoes. Transfer to a heated 9-inch (23 cm) skillet. Add 1 Tablespoon olive oil and sauté tomatoes until heated through, 1 to 2 minutes. Remove from heat and add 1 Tablespoon chopped fennel fronds. Season to taste with salt and ground black pepper. Remove to a container and set aside.

6. Place fennel, zucchini, and onion mixture into the Vitamix container and secure lid.

7. Select Variable 1.

8. Switch machine to Start and slowly increase speed to Variable 10.

9. Blend for 30 seconds.

10. Return to saucepan and heat over medium heat until hot. Serve soup garnished with warm tomato garnish. Season to taste with sea salt, if desired.

Nutritional Information

Amount Per Serving: *Calories 140, Total Fat 10g, Saturated Fat 1.5g, Cholesterol 0mg, Sodium 40mg, Total Carbohydrates 12g, Dietary Fiber 4g, Sugars 4g, Protein 2g*

Dairy-free

Gluten-free

Tomato Thyme Soup

Preparation: 20 minutes | **Processing:** 6 minutes 30 seconds
Yield: 5 ½ cups (1.3 l) (5 servings)

1 ½ cups (360 ml) water

1 (14 ½-ounce/410 g) can diced tomatoes

2 Roma tomatoes, halved

1 medium carrot, halved

¾ cup (75 g) oil packed sun dried tomatoes, drained

1 teaspoon flaxseed

1 ½ Tablespoons chopped onion

1 garlic clove, peeled

½ Tablespoon fresh thyme sprigs (leaves only if sprigs are woody and thick)

1 teaspoon fresh oregano leaves

1 Tablespoon tomato paste

½ vegetable bouillon cube

½ cup (120 ml) whole milk, room temperature

Chef's Note

Sun-dried tomatoes *are a great source of rich, unique flavor brought out through a slow aging process. Add them to the top of the finished soup for a mouthwatering garnish.*

1. Place water, canned tomatoes, fresh tomatoes, carrot, sun dried tomatoes, flaxseed, onion, garlic, thyme, oregano, tomato paste, and bouillon into the Vitamix container in the order listed and secure lid.

2. Select Variable 1.

3. Switch machine to Start and slowly increase speed to Variable 10.

4. Blend for 6 minutes.

5. Reduce speed to Variable 2 and remove lid plug.

6. Slowly add milk through the lid plug opening. Replace lid plug.

7. Slowly increase speed to Variable 10 and blend for an additional 30 seconds.

Nutritional Information

Amount Per Serving: *Calories 90, Total Fat 3.5g, Saturated Fat 1g, Cholesterol 5mg, Sodium 450mg, Total Carbohydrate 13g, Dietary Fiber 3g, Sugars 6g, Protein 3g*

Vegetarian

Broccoli Cheese Soup

Preparation: 15 minutes | **Processing:** 5 minutes 45 seconds
Yield: 2 ¼ cups (540 ml) (2 servings)

1 cup (240 ml) milk

½ cup (56 g) shredded Cheddar cheese

2 cups (312 g) steamed broccoli, divided use

1 teaspoon diced onion

½ chicken bouillon cube

1. Place milk, cheese, 1 ½ cups broccoli, onion, and bouillon into the Vitamix container in the order listed and secure lid.

2. Select Variable 1.

3. Switch machine to Start and slowly increase speed to Variable 10.

4. Blend for 5 minutes 45 seconds or until steam escapes from the vented lid.

5. Place ¼ cup (39 g) steamed broccoli in each bowl. Pour soup over broccoli and serve.

Nutritional Information

Amount Per Serving: *Calories 250, Total Fat 14g, Saturated Fat 8g, Cholesterol 40mg, Sodium 530mg, Total Carbohydrate 18g, Dietary Fiber 5g, Sugars 8g, Protein 15g*

Leafy Green Soup

Preparation: 20 minutes | ***Processing:*** 40–60 seconds | ***Cook Time:*** 1 hour
Yield: 9 ½ cups (2.2 l) (9 servings)

2 Tablespoons (30 ml)
extra virgin olive oil

9 ounces (255 g) yellow
onion, rough chopped

1 teaspoon salt, divided use

2 Tablespoons (30 ml) plus
3 cups (720 ml) water,
divided use

¼ cup (48 g) uncooked
Arborio rice

1 bunch, 1 pound (454 g)
green chard, white ribs
removed, rough chopped

14 cups (420 g) gently
packed spinach leaves,
rough chopped

4 cups (960 ml) Homemade
Vegetable Stock (page 162)

Large pinch of
cayenne pepper

1 Tablespoon lemon juice

1. Heat oil in a large skillet over high heat. Add onions and ¼ teaspoon salt; cook, stirring frequently until the onions begin to brown, about 5 minutes. Reduce heat to low, add 2 Tablespoons (30 ml) water and cover. Cook, stirring frequently until the pan cools down, then occasionally, always covering the pan, until the onions reduce and have a deep caramel color, 25 to 30 minutes.

2. Combine 3 cups (720 ml) water and ¾ teaspoon salt in a Dutch oven. Add rice and bring to a boil. Reduce heat; cover and simmer for 15 minutes. Stir in chard, return to a simmer, cover and cook for 10 minutes. Add cooked onions, spinach, broth, and cayenne. Return to a simmer, cover and cook, stirring once until spinach is tender, 5 minutes.

3. Place half the mixture into the Vitamix container and secure lid.

4. Select Variable 1.

5. Switch machine to Start and slowly increase speed to Variable 10.

6. Blend for 20 to 30 seconds. Pour into a soup pot and repeat with remaining half of mixture. Heat over medium heat until hot. Stir in 1 Tablespoon lemon juice prior to serving.

Nutritional Information

Amount Per Serving: *Calories 90, Total Fat 3g, Saturated Fat 0g, Cholesterol 0mg, Sodium 440mg, Total Carbohydrates 14g, Dietary Fiber 4g, Sugars 2g, Protein 3g*

Vegan

Vegetarian

Dairy-free

Gluten-free

Chestnut Soup

Preparation: 20 minutes | **Processing:** 35–40 seconds
Cook Time: 35 minutes | **Yield:** 8 cups (1.9 l) (8 servings)

Soup:

2 Tablespoons (28 g)
unsalted butter

1 medium onion, 4 ounces
(114 g), rough chopped

1 stalk celery, 3 ounces (85 g),
rough chopped

1 medium carrot, 3 ½ ounces
(99 g), rough chopped

1 garlic clove, peeled

4 cups (960 ml) Homemade
Vegetable Stock (page 162)

2 cups (480 ml) water

1 bay leaf

1 (15-ounce/425 g) jar
roasted chestnuts, drained

Sea salt, to taste

Croutons (optional):

3 Tablespoons (42 g)
unsalted butter

2 cups (256 g) cubed rustic
bread, crusts removed
(see note)

½ teaspoon saffron threads

Chef's Note

"Rustic bread" is a term used to describe artisanal breads that are made without loaf pans. They usually have crisp crusts and chewy interiors, such as Italian and French breads.

1. Melt the 2 Tablespoons (28 g) butter in a large saucepan over medium heat. Add the onion, celery, and carrot. Cook until soft, about 8 minutes. Add garlic and cook until aromatic, about 30 seconds.

2. Add vegetable stock, water, and bay leaf. Bring to a boil, then reduce heat to medium-low and simmer 5 minutes.

3. Add chestnuts and simmer until chestnuts and vegetables are tender, about 10 minutes. Remove bay leaf.

4. Carefully ladle cooked mixture into the Vitamix container and secure lid.

5. Select Variable 1.

6. Switch machine to Start and slowly increase speed to Variable 10.

7. Blend for 35 to 40 seconds.

Chestnut Soup continues on page 128

continued from page 126

Chestnut Soup

8. Pour into a large saucepan and bring up to temperature over medium heat.

9. Meanwhile, melt 3 Tablespoons (42 g) butter in a skillet over medium heat. Add the bread and cook, stirring until golden, about 3 minutes. Add the saffron and cook until the croutons are browned.

10. Ladle soup into bowls and garnish with croutons. Season to taste with salt, if desired.

Nutritional Information

Amount Per Serving (with croutons): *Calories 170, Total Fat 8g, Saturated Fat 5g, Cholesterol 20mg, Sodium 80mg, Total Carbohydrates 22g, Dietary Fiber 1g, Sugars 2g, Protein 2g*

Vegetarian

Winter Squash Soup

Preparation: 30 minutes | **Processing:** 35–40 seconds
Cook Time: 20–25 minutes | **Yield:** 6 ¼ cups (1.5 l) (6 servings)

1 Tablespoon olive oil

1 medium onion, 4 ½ ounces (128 g), chopped

2 garlic cloves, peeled and halved

2 teaspoons smoked paprika

1 bay leaf

2 Tablespoons (30 ml) dry sherry

1 ½ pounds (680 g) winter squash, peeled, seeded, and cut into 1-inch (2.5 cm) pieces

2 cups (480 ml) Homemade Vegetable Stock (page 162)

1 cup (240 ml) water

Sea salt, to taste

Chef's Note

Always select winter squash that seem heavy for their size. Look for clean, thick skin with no scuffs or blemishes. For the squash to keep well, you want a piece of the stem to still be attached, and the skin should not give when pressed.

1. Heat oil in a large pot over medium-high heat. Add onion, sauté for 3 to 5 minutes, then stir in garlic, smoked paprika, and bay leaf. Cook for 1 minute.

2. Add sherry, cook 2 minutes. Add squash, broth, and water. Bring to a simmer, cover, and reduce heat to medium-low. Cook 20 minutes, or until squash is tender. Remove bay leaf.

3. Carefully place hot mixture into the Vitamix container and secure lid.

4. Select Variable 1.

5. Switch machine to Start and slowly increase speed to Variable 10.

6. Blend for 35 to 40 seconds.

7. Season to taste with sea salt, if desired.

Nutritional Information

Amount Per Serving: *Calories 70, Total Fat 2.5g, Saturated Fat 0g, Cholesterol 0mg, Sodium 10mg, Total Carbohydrate 13g, Dietary Fiber 2g, Sugars 4g, Protein 2g*

 Vegan   **Vegetarian**   **Dairy-free**   **Gluten-free**

Winter Greens Soup

Preparation: 20 minutes | **Processing:** 1 minute plus pulsing
Cook Time: 25–30 minutes | **Yield:** 11 ½ cups (2.8 l) (11 servings)

2 leeks, trimmed, halved, and sliced

2 stalks celery, 4 ½ ounces (128 g), chopped

2 garlic cloves, peeled

1 cup (240 ml) water

5 ¼ cups (1.2 l) Homemade Vegetable Stock (page 162)

1 (14 ½-ounce/410 g) can no salt added diced tomatoes

4 cups (268 g) chopped kale

17 ½ ounces (497 g) zucchini, halved and sliced

¼ teaspoon ground black pepper

5 ounces (142 g) fresh baby spinach

½ cup (30 g) Italian parsley or basil leaves

2 Tablespoons (30 ml) red wine vinegar

chopped tomato, for garnish

chopped basil, for garnish

Sea salt, to taste

Chef's Note

You can buy pre-chopped kale in large bags in the produce section. Use leftover kale in your favorite green smoothie, combining a small amount with spinach or other leafy greens at first, and increasing the kale gradually to allow your taste buds to adjust to the bolder flavor.

1. In a large Dutch oven, sauté leeks, celery, and garlic in a few Tablespoons of water over medium heat. Sauté for 10 minutes or until softened, stirring frequently. Continue to add water, a few Tablespoons at a time, as needed to prevent the vegetables from sticking. Stir in broth, tomatoes, kale, zucchini, and pepper. Bring to a boil. Reduce heat and simmer covered, 5 minutes, stirring once.

2. Place half of the mixture into the Vitamix container and secure lid. Select Variable 1.

3. Switch machine to Start and slowly increase speed to Variable 10. Blend for 30 seconds. Pour into a clean pot.

4. Repeat with remaining soup. After blending, remove lid and add fresh spinach, parsley, and vinegar and secure lid. Select Variable 6.

5. Pulse 5 times. Pour into pot containing other blended soup. Heat over medium heat until hot. Ladle soup into bowls and garnish with chopped tomatoes and basil. Season to taste with sea salt, if desired.

Nutritional Information

Amount Per Serving: Calories 50, Total Fat 0.5g, Saturated Fat 0g, Cholesterol 0mg, Sodium 55mg, Total Carbohydrate 10g, Dietary Fiber 3g, Sugars 2g, Protein 3g

Vegan **Vegetarian** **Dairy-free** **Gluten-free**

Basic Sweet Potato Soup

Preparation: 25 minutes | **Processing:** 5 minutes 55 seconds
Cook Time: 10 minutes | **Yield:** 6 cups (1.4 l) (6 servings)

4 cups (960 ml) Homemade
Chicken or Vegetable Stock
(page 162–163)

1 pound (454 g)
sweet potatoes

3 Tablespoons (45 ml)
orange juice

½ teaspoon orange zest

¼ teaspoon ground nutmeg

¼ cup (60 ml) half & half

Sea salt, to taste

Chef's Note

If you don't *have store-
bought vegetable or
chicken stock on hand, it's
easy to create a quick,
flavorful stock for your
soups (see Soups).
The type of stock you
choose to use in your
recipes is based entirely on
preference as vegetable
and chicken or beef stock
are interchangeable.*

1. Pierce sweet potatoes several times with a knife and place in microwave.
   Cook on High for 7 to 10 minutes or until fork tender. Remove from microwave
   and let cool. Peel and quarter potatoes.

2. Place chicken broth, sweet potatoes, orange juice, orange zest, and nutmeg
   into the Vitamix container and secure lid.

3. Select Variable 1.

4. Switch machine to Start and slowly increase speed to Variable 10.

5. Blend for 5 minutes 45 seconds. Reduce speed to Variable 2 and remove the lid plug.

6. Add half & half through the lid plug opening. Replace lid plug and blend
   an additional 10 seconds.

7. Season to taste with sea salt, if desired.

Nutritional Information

Amount Per Serving: *Calories 90, Total Fat 1.5g, Saturated Fat 1g, Cholesterol 5mg,
Sodium 35mg, Total Carbohydrates 17g, Dietary Fiber 3g, Sugars 6g, Protein 2g*

Gluten-free

Lemony Leek Soup

Preparation: 25 minutes | ***Processing:*** 30 – 45 seconds
Cook Time: 30 minutes | ***Yield:*** 6 ½ cups (1.5 l) (6 servings)

2 Tablespoons (30 ml) olive oil

6 ½ cups (579 g) thinly sliced leeks, white and pale green parts only

4 ounces (114 g) Russet potato, quartered

4 cups (960 ml) Homemade Vegetable Stock (page 162)

3 Tablespoons (9 g) fresh dill, divided use

¼ teaspoon fresh grated nutmeg

¼ cup (60 g) plain yogurt

1 Tablespoon lemon zest

Sea salt and ground black pepper, to taste

Dill sprigs, for garnish

1. Heat olive oil in a large, heavy-bottom pot over medium heat. Add leeks and cook until softened and wilted, stirring often, 5 to 6 minutes.

2. Add potato, stir to coat. Add broth and bring to a boil. Reduce heat to medium and simmer until vegetables are tender, about 15 minutes.

3. Place mixture into the Vitamix container. Add nutmeg and 2 Tablespoons (6 g) dill and secure lid.

4. Select Variable 1.

5. Switch machine to Start and slowly increase speed to Variable 10.

6. Blend for 30 to 45 seconds.

7. Before serving, whisk lemon zest and 1 Tablespoon chopped dill into the plain yogurt. Season to taste with salt and pepper.

8. Divide soup into 6 bowls and garnish with a dollop of yogurt sauce and fresh dill.

Nutritional Information

Amount Per Serving: *Calories 120, Total Fat 5g, Saturated Fat 1g, Cholesterol 0mg, Sodium 35mg, Total Carbohydrates 19g, Dietary Fiber 2g, Sugars 5g, Protein 3g*

Vegetarian **Gluten-free**

Acorn Squash Soup

Preparation: 15 minutes | **Processing:** 6 minutes
Yield: 4 cups (960 ml) (4 servings)

2 cups (480 ml) Homemade
Vegetable Stock (page 162)

1 medium acorn squash, seeded,
roasted, and peeled, about
2 cups (490 g) mashed

2 teaspoons maple syrup

pinch ground nutmeg

½ teaspoon ground cinnamon

Sea salt and ground black
pepper, to taste

1. Place stock, squash, maple syrup, nutmeg, and cinnamon into
   the Vitamix container in the order listed and secure lid.

2. Select Variable 1.

3. Switch machine to Start and slowly increase speed to Variable 10.

4. Blend for 6 minutes.

5. Season to taste with salt and pepper, if desired.

Nutritional Information

Amount Per Serving: *Calories 50, Total Fat 0g, Saturated Fat 0g,
Cholesterol 0mg, Sodium 10mg, Total Carbohydrate 14g,
Dietary Fiber 3g, Sugars 2g, Protein 1g*

Vegan   **Vegetarian**   **Dairy-free**   **Gluten-free**

Chef's Note

To save time, *cut squash in
half, remove seeds, and
place face down in a
microwaveable dish. Add
water to cover the bottom
of the dish. Cover and
microwave on High until
tender, about 7 minutes.
Let cool and scoop
out flesh.*

Ingredient IQ

Produce at its Peak

Fresh produce tastes best —
and has the most nutrients
— when grown, picked, and
served at its peak. You'll find
the freshest at your local
farmer's market. Growing
seasons differ by region,
but here are some seasonal
highlights that make the
perfect ingredients for
a homemade soup:

Winter: kale, chard, cabbage,
onions (white, red or yellow)

Spring: spinach, cucumber,
lettuce, green onions

Summer: fresh herbs (mint,
basil, parsley), bell peppers,
tomatoes, zucchini

Fall: sweet potatoes,
potatoes, winter squash

Beet Soup

Preparation: 15 minutes | *Processing:* 1 minute | *Cook Time:* 30 minutes
Yield: 5 cups (1.2 l) (5 servings)

1 cup (240 ml) water

2 garlic cloves, peeled
and chopped

4 ounces (114 g) Russet
potato, quartered

2 (15-ounce/425 g)
cans beets, drained

3 ½ cups (840 ml) Homemade
Vegetable Stock (page 162)

1 Tablespoon fresh dill, plus
additional for garnish

⅛ teaspoon ground black pepper

Vegan Sour Cream (page 186)

Sea salt, to taste

1. In a heated saucepan, sauté garlic in a few Tablespoons of water over medium heat for 1 minute. Add potato and continue to add water, a few Tablespoons at a time, as needed to prevent sticking. Cook for 5 minutes, stirring frequently. Add beets and chicken broth; bring to a boil. Reduce heat, cover, and simmer for 20 minutes.

2. Carefully place hot beet mixture, fresh dill, and pepper into the Vitamix container and secure lid.

3. Select Variable 1.

4. Switch machine to Start and slowly increase speed to Variable 10.

5. Blend for 1 minute. Ladle into bowls and garnish with Vegan Sour Cream and dill sprig. Season to taste with sea salt, if desired.

Nutritional Information

Amount Per Serving: Calories 70, Total Fat 0g, Saturated Fat 0g, Cholesterol 0mg, Sodium 45mg, Total Carbohydrate 16g, Dietary Fiber 2g, Sugars 9g, Protein 2g

Vegan   **Vegetarian**   **Dairy-free**   **Gluten-free**

Sweet Potato Broccoli Soup

Preparation: 20 minutes | ***Processing:*** 1 minute | ***Cook Time:*** 30 minutes
Yield: 7 ¾ cups (1.8 l) (7 servings)

2 Tablespoons (30 ml) extra
virgin olive oil

1 medium onion, 3 ½ ounces
(99 g), rough chopped

2 stalks celery, 6 ounces (170 g),
rough chopped

2 cups (480 ml) Homemade Chicken
or Vegetable Stock (page 162–163)

1 cup (240 ml) half & half

½ pound (227 g) Russet
potatoes, quartered

1 pound (454 g) sweet potatoes,
peeled and quartered (about 3–6
sweet potatoes)

1 bay leaf

1 cup (240 ml) water

Kosher salt, to taste

Ground black pepper, to taste

3 cups (213 g) broccoli florets

3 Tablespoons (45 ml) water

1 ⅓ cups, ⅓ pound (151 g)
shredded sharp Cheddar

1. Heat olive oil in a large pot over medium-high heat. Add onion and celery and cook, stirring until softened, about 5 minutes. Add broth, half & half, Russet and sweet potatoes, bay leaf, water, salt, and black pepper; bring to a boil.

2. Reduce heat to medium-low and simmer until the potatoes are tender, about 10 minutes. Meanwhile, put the broccoli in a microwave safe bowl, add 3 Tablespoons (45 ml) water, cover and microwave on High 4 minutes, or until crisp tender.

3. When potatoes are tender, remove from heat, and let cool 10 minutes. Remove bay leaf.

4. Carefully place hot mixture into the Vitamix container and secure lid. Select Variable 1. Switch machine to Start and slowly increase speed to Variable 10. Blend for 1 minute.

5. Return to pot and heat over medium heat until hot. Add broccoli and Cheddar cheese. Stir until cheese is melted. Season to taste with kosher salt, if desired.

Nutritional Information

Amount Per Serving: *Calories 230, Total Fat 12g, Saturated Fat 5g, Cholesterol 25mg, Sodium 200mg, Total Carbohydrates 23g, Dietary Fiber 4g, Sugars 4g, Protein 9g*

Gluten-free

Sweet Potato Sage Soup

Preparation: 35 minutes | **Processing:** 1 minute 15 seconds
Cook Time: 1 hour | **Yield:** 11 ½ cups (2.8 l) (11 servings)

3 Tablespoons (45 ml) extra virgin olive oil, divided use

1 cup (160 g) diced onion

1 teaspoon salt, divided use

2 Tablespoons (30 ml) plus 4 cups (960 ml) water, divided use

4 garlic cloves, peeled and halved

1 teaspoon chopped fresh thyme leaves

1 large bunch kale, tough stems removed, rough chopped

1 pound (454 g) sweet potatoes, peeled and cut into 1-inch (2.5 cm) cubes

8 fresh sage leaves

12 ounces (340 g) fresh spinach

4 cups (960 ml) Homemade Vegetable Stock (page 162)

Pinch of cayenne pepper

Pinch of ground black pepper

1 Tablespoon fresh lemon juice

1 Tablespoon honey

1. Heat 2 Tablespoons (30 ml) oil in a skillet over high heat. Add onion and ¼ teaspoon salt. Cook, stirring frequently, until the onions begin to brown, about 5 minutes. Reduce heat to low, stir in 2 Tablespoons (30 ml) water, garlic, and thyme. Cover and cook, stirring frequently until the pan cools down, then occasionally, always covering the pan, until the onions reduce and have a deep caramel color, 25 to 30 minutes.

2. Meanwhile, combine 4 cups (960 ml) water and ¾ teaspoon salt in a Dutch oven; add kale, sweet potato, and sage. Bring to a boil. Reduce heat to maintain a simmer; cover and cook 15 minutes.

3. Stir in spinach, return to a simmer, cover and cook for 10 additional minutes. When the onions are caramelized, stir a little simmering liquid into them. Scrape the bottom of the skillet to incorporate any browned bits, and add mixture to the soup. Add vegetable broth, return to a simmer. Cook 5 additional minutes.

4. Place half the mixture into the Vitamix container and secure lid.

5. Select Variable 1.

Sweet Potato Sage Soup continues on page 140

Dried Herbs vs. Fresh Herbs

Both fresh and dried herbs can add robust flavor to the simplest of dishes, but it's important to know when it's best to use dried versus fresh. Dried herbs are best if added during the cooking process, which allows time to infuse flavor into the dish. Fresh herbs, on the other hand, are ideal for finishing a dish.

Herbs such as oregano, thyme, and rosemary tend to retain flavor when dried. Softer, herbs like basil and chives lose much of their flavor when they're dried, making them perfect garnishes.

A general rule of thumb is to use 1 ½ times the amount of fresh herbs as you would dry herbs when substituting in a recipe. Because dried herbs have a more concentrated flavor, use a smaller amount than you would fresh herbs and adjust flavors as needed.

continued from page 139

Sweet Potato Sage Soup

6. Switch machine to Start and slowly increase speed to Variable 8.

7. Blend for 35 to 40 seconds. Pour into a clean soup pot and repeat with remaining half. Stir in cayenne, ground black pepper, lemon juice, and honey.

Nutritional Information

Amount Per Serving: *Calories 110, Total Fat 4.5g, Saturated Fat 0.5g, Cholesterol 0mg, Sodium 270mg, Total Carbohydrate 16g, Dietary Fiber 3g, Sugars 4g, Protein 3g*

Vegetarian

Dairy-free

Gluten-free

Cream of Asparagus Soup

Preparation: 25 minutes | ***Processing:*** 3 minutes 30 seconds
Cook Time: 10 minutes | ***Yield:*** 4 ½ cups (1.0 l) (4 servings)

1 ½ pounds (680 g) asparagus spears,
trimmed of woody ends, divided use

1 ½ cups (360 ml) Homemade
Vegetable Stock (page 162)

⅛ teaspoon sea salt

⅛ teaspoon ground black pepper

1. Steam asparagus in a small amount of water until tender, about 10 minutes.
   Drain. Set aside 1 cup (180 g) asparagus pieces for garnish.

2. Place asparagus, stock, salt, and pepper into the Vitamix
   container and secure lid.

3. Select Variable 1.

4. Switch machine to Start and slowly increase speed to Variable 10.

5. Blend for 3 minutes 30 seconds or until heavy steam escapes from the vented lid.

6. Serve immediately over reserved asparagus pieces.

Nutritional Information

Amount Per Serving: *Calories 40, Total Fat 0g, Saturated Fat 0g, Cholesterol 0mg,
Sodium 85mg, Total Carbohydrate 7g, Dietary Fiber 3g, Sugars 2g, Protein 4g*

Vegan **Vegetarian** **Dairy-free** **Gluten-free**

Chef's Note

Fresh herbs *such as
parsley, basil, or chervil
impart extra flavor when
added as a garnish,
allowing you to adjust the
taste of creamy soups
without adding extra salt.*

Leek, Artichoke and Potato Soup

Preparation: 20 minutes | **Processing:** 30–40 seconds
Cook Time: 35–40 minutes | **Yield:** 7 ½ cups (1.8 l) (7 servings)

2 Tablespoons (30 ml) olive oil

2 medium leeks, 2 cups (180 g), white parts chopped

9 garlic cloves, peeled

2 cups (480 ml) Homemade Vegetable Stock (page 162)

2 (9.9-ounce/281 g) jars artichoke hearts in water, rinsed and drained

6 ounces (170 g) Russet potatoes, cut into 1-inch (2.5 cm) chunks

6 fresh thyme sprigs, stemmed

2 cups (480 ml) water

2 teaspoons lemon juice

6 Tablespoons (90 g) Kale and Basil Pesto (page 252)

Sea salt, to taste

Chef's Note

To make this soup vegan, simply omit the cheese in the pesto, or omit the pesto entirely.

1. Heat oil in a large saucepan over medium heat. Add leeks and garlic; sauté for 5 minutes or until leeks are softened and translucent. Add broth, artichokes, potatoes, thyme leaves, and 2 cups (480 ml) water. Cover and bring to a boil.

2. Reduce heat to medium-low; simmer partially covered for 20 to 25 minutes or until potatoes are tender.

3. Place mixture into the Vitamix container. Add lemon juice and secure lid.

4. Select Variable 1.

5. Switch machine to Start and slowly increase speed to Variable 10.

6. Blend for 30 to 40 seconds.

7. Divide into bowls and garnish with Kale Basil Pesto. Season to taste with sea salt, if desired.

Nutritional Information

Amount Per Serving: Calories 180, Total Fat 11g, Saturated Fat 1.5g, Cholesterol 5mg, Sodium 330mg, Total Carbohydrates 15g, Dietary Fiber 1g, Sugars 2g, Protein 5g

Vegetarian

Dairy-free

Gluten-free

Crab Bisque

Preparation: 25 minutes | **Processing:** Pulsing plus 30–40 seconds
Cook Time: 30–35 minutes | **Yield:** 4 ¾ cups (1.1 l) soup and
2 cups (480 ml) relish (4 servings)

Chef's Note

A bisque is a type of soup that is typically made with shellfish such as lobster, crab, shrimp, or crayfish. Traditionally, rice is used as a thickening agent. Although classic bisques are made only with shellfish, thicker, vegetable-based soups and soups with meat are sometimes referred to as bisques.

Relish:

1 medium tomato, 5 ounces
(142 g), quartered

1 cup (154 g) fresh corn kernels
or frozen, thawed

1 small avocado, pitted, peeled

1 Tablespoon lime juice

¼ teaspoon salt

Dash of ground black pepper

Bisque:

1 Tablespoon extra virgin
olive oil

1 cup (154 g) fresh corn kernels
or frozen, thawed

1 cup (160 g) chopped onion

1 cup (150 g) chopped yellow
bell pepper

1 ½ cups (225 g) unpeeled and
chopped Russet potato

¾ teaspoon sweet or
hot smoked paprika, plus
additional for garnish

1 cup (240 ml) dry sherry

2 cups (480 ml) clam juice

2 cups (480 ml) 2% milk

12 ounces (340 g) crab
meat, rinsed

½ teaspoon salt

1. Place tomato, corn, avocado, lime juice, salt, and pepper into the Vitamix container in the order listed and secure lid.

2. Select Variable 1.

3. Pulse 3 to 4 times. Stop machine and remove lid. Scrape down the sides of the container with a spatula and secure lid. Repeat process until desired consistency is reached. Set aside.

4. Heat oil in a large saucepan over medium heat. Add corn, onion, bell pepper and cook, stirring often, until the onion and pepper have softened, about 5 minutes.

5. Add potato and paprika and cook, stirring often, for 2 minutes. Add sherry and cook, scraping the bottom of the skillet to incorporate brown bits until the liquid has reduced slightly, about 5 minutes. Add clam juice and bring to a boil. Reduce heat and simmer, until the potatoes are tender, about 15 minutes. Remove from heat and let cool 15 minutes.

Crab Bisque continues on page 146

continued from page 145

Crab Bisque

6. Place mixture into the Vitamix container and secure lid.

7. Select Variable 1.

8. Switch machine to Start and slowly increase speed to Variable 10.

9. Blend for 30 to 40 seconds.

10. Return purée to the saucepan. Stir in milk and crab meat. Cook, stirring occasionally, until heated through, 3 to 5 minutes.

11. Serve topped with relish and sprinkled with paprika.

Nutritional Information

Amount Per Serving: *Calories 460, Total Fat 13g, Saturated Fat 3g, Cholesterol 80mg, Sodium 1260mg, Total Carbohydrates 45g, Dietary Fiber 6g, Sugars 18g, Protein 25g*

Gluten-free

White Onion Apple Soup

Preparation: 25 minutes | **Processing:** 30–40 seconds
Cook Time: 30 minutes | **Yield:** 7 cups (1.7 l) (7 servings)

½ cup (120 ml) water, divided use

1 ½ cups (240 g) chopped white onion

1 ¼ pounds (568 g) carrots, quartered

3 ¾ cups (900 ml) Homemade Chicken Stock (page 163)

1 Fuji apple, cored and quartered, divided use

2 teaspoons chopped fresh ginger root

4 ½ Tablespoons (68 ml) frozen apple juice concentrate, thawed

¼ teaspoon fresh grated nutmeg

¼ teaspoon ground allspice

Kosher salt and ground black pepper, to taste

chopped fresh mint

1. Preheat a large saucepan over medium-high heat. Add onion and a few Tablespoons of water. Sauté 2 minutes, stirring frequently. Add additional water, a few Tablespoons at a time, as needed to prevent sticking. Add carrots, broth, 2 apple quarters, and ginger. Bring to a boil. Cover and reduce heat. Simmer until carrots are tender, 20 minutes.

2. Carefully place hot soup mixture into the Vitamix container, add apple juice, nutmeg, and allspice and secure lid. Select Variable 1.

3. Switch machine to Start and slowly increase speed to Variable 10.

4. Blend for 30 to 40 seconds.

5. Season to taste with salt and pepper. Dice remaining apple quarters. Ladle soup into bowls and garnish with diced apple and mint.

Nutritional Information

Amount Per Serving: *Calories 80, Total Fat 0g, Saturated Fat 0g, Cholesterol 0mg, Sodium 60mg, Total Carbohydrate 20g, Dietary Fiber 4g, Sugars 13g, Protein 1g*

Dairy-free **Gluten-free**

Healthy Choices

Sauté with Water

With a non-stick pan and a little water, you can easily sauté vegetables without the use of fattening olive oil or butter. Simply heat 2 to 3 Tablespoons of water in a pan and sauté as usual. Vegetables such as onions, celery, and garlic are high in water content and need very little (if any) additional water to prevent them from sticking to the pan.

When a fork is easily inserted through your vegetables, remove from heat and serve or incorporate into your recipe.

Curried Cauliflower Soup

Preparation: 20 minutes | ***Processing:*** 45–50 seconds
Cook Time: 30 minutes | ***Yield:*** 7 ½ cups (1.8 l) (7 servings)

1 cup (240 ml) water,
divided use

1 medium onion, 5 ounces
(142 g), rough chopped

1 medium tart apple, 7 ounces
(200 g), cored and quartered,
plus additional for garnish

1 Tablespoon curry powder

1 garlic clove, peeled

1 large head, 6 cups (600 g)
cauliflower, chopped into
1-inch (2.5 cm) pieces

4 cups (960 ml) Homemade
Vegetable Stock (page 162)

1 teaspoon honey

1 teaspoon rice wine vinegar

Sea salt, to taste

Chef's Note

Soup can easily *become
a shareable appetizer
when served as shooters.
Pour homemade soup
into tall, 2-ounce shot
glasses and garnish with
a sprig of rosemary
for a lovely presentation.*

1. Heat a large pot over medium-high heat. Add onion and a few Tablespoons of water. Sauté 5 to 7 minutes or until soft and golden, stirring frequently. Continue to add water, a few Tablespoons at a time, as needed to prevent the onions from sticking. Stir in apple, curry powder, and garlic. Cook an additional 2 minutes until curry turns deep yellow.

2. Add cauliflower and broth and bring to a simmer. Cover, reduce heat to medium-low, and simmer 20 minutes.

3. Place mixture into the Vitamix container and secure lid. Select Variable 1.

4. Switch machine to Start and slowly increase speed to Variable 8. Blend for 35 to 40 seconds.

5. Reduce speed to Variable 1 and remove lid plug.

6. Pour honey and vinegar through the lid plug opening. Replace lid plug and blend an additional 10 seconds.

7. Dice an additional apple quarter or two. Ladle soup into bowls and garnish with diced apple. Season to taste with sea salt, if desired.

Nutritional Information

Amount Per Serving: *Calories 60, Total Fat 0g, Saturated Fat 0g, Cholesterol 0mg, Sodium 35mg, Total Carbohydrate 12g, Dietary Fiber 3g, Sugars 7g, Protein 2g*

Vegetarian **Dairy-free** **Gluten-free**

Gazpacho

Preparation: 20 minutes | ***Processing:*** 10 seconds plus Pulsing
Chill Time: 1–2 hours | ***Yield:*** 6 cups (1.4 l) (6 servings)

1 garlic clove, peeled

1 ½ pounds (680 g) ripe tomatoes, quartered, divided use

½ pound (227 g) cucumber, divided use

½ green bell pepper, quartered, divided use

2 scallions, white and light green parts only, divided use

¼ jalapeño, seeded

¼ cup (15 g) flat leaf parsley

2 Tablespoons (11 g) fresh mint leaves

1 Tablespoon sherry vinegar

1 ½ cups (360 ml) tomato juice

Sea salt and ground black pepper, to taste

1. Place garlic, half of the tomatoes, half of the cucumber, half of the bell pepper, half of the scallions, and jalapeño into the Vitamix container in the order listed and secure lid.

2. Select Variable 1.

3. Switch machine to Start and slowly increase speed to Variable 5.

4. Blend for 10 seconds. Transfer to a large bowl.

5. Add parsley, mint, vinegar, tomato juice, and black pepper into the Vitamix container in the order listed and secure lid.

6. Select Variable 1.

7. Pulse 5 to 6 times. Increase speed to Variable 2 and continue Pulsing if desired to obtain finer consistency. Add to the gazpacho in a large bowl. Chill for 1 to 2 hours before serving. Season to taste with sea salt and pepper.

Nutritional Information

Amount Per Serving: *Calories 45, Total Fat 0g, Saturated Fat 0g, Cholesterol 0mg, Sodium 200mg, Total Carbohydrate 10g, Dietary Fiber 2g, Sugars 6g, Protein 2g*

Vegan **Vegetarian** **Dairy-free** **Gluten-free**

Clam Chowder

Preparation: 20 minutes | **Processing:** 30 seconds
Cook Time: 40 minutes | **Yield:** 6 ½ cups (1.5 l) (6 servings)

Chef's Note

Look for low-sodium clam juice to avoid unwanted salt.

2 cups (480 ml) clam juice

2 pounds (908 g) chopped clam meat, rinsed

10 ounces (284 g) Russet potatoes cut into ½-inch (1.3 cm) cubes

1 slice bacon, chopped

1 medium onion, 5 ounces (142 g), rough chopped

1 stalk celery, 3 ounces (85 g), rough chopped

2 bay leaves

2 garlic cloves, peeled, rough chopped

1 teaspoon fresh thyme

1 cup (240 ml) half & half

6 teaspoons unsalted butter, sliced into 6 pats

2 Tablespoons (8 g) chopped fresh parsley

2 Tablespoons (6 g) chopped fresh chives

½ teaspoon paprika

1. Bring 2 cups (480 ml) clam juice and clams to a simmer. Remove clams with a slotted spoon and set aside.

2. Add potatoes to the clam juice and simmer until tender, about 10 to 15 minutes. Remove from heat. Cool 15 minutes.

3. While potatoes are cooking, sauté bacon over medium heat until crisp. Add onion, celery, and bay leaves; cook until soft, about 3 minutes. Add garlic and thyme; cook 3 minutes. Cool slightly and remove bay leaves.

4. Place ⅓ of the potatoes, simmering liquid, and cooked vegetables into the Vitamix container and secure lid.

5. Select Variable 1.

6. Switch machine to Start and slowly increase speed to Variable 7.

7. Blend for 30 seconds.

Clam Chowder *continues on page 152*

Planning Ahead

Stock Your Freezer

When you're strapped for time or don't feel like cooking, a freezer stocked with homemade soup is a lifesaver.

Remember to only freeze soup in packages sized for single use, whether that's a cup for a quick lunch or a quart for a quick family meal. Stored in an airtight container, most soups can be frozen for up to two months. For best results, place frozen, quart-size containers in the fridge to thaw for 24 hours before preparing.

Avoid freezing soups that include cream. Instead, freeze the soup then reheat and add cream right before serving.

If you're running out the door and realize you forgot to pack a lunch, grab one of those single-serving containers and let it thaw in the fridge at work until heating at lunchtime.

continued from page 151

Clam Chowder

8. Return to pot, add clam meat, reserved potato, and stir in half & half. Heat on medium-low heat for 15 minutes.

9. Pour into bowls and garnish with a pat of butter, parsley, chives, and paprika.

Nutritional Information

Amount Per Serving: *Calories 280, Total Fat 11g, Saturated Fat 6g, Cholesterol 75mg, Sodium 867mg, Total Carbohydrates 19g, Dietary Fiber 1g, Sugars 2g, Protein 26g*

Gluten-free

Simple Tomato Soup

Preparation: 15 minutes | *Processing:* 6 minutes 30 seconds | *Yield:* 5 cups (1.2 l) (5 servings)

2 (14 ½-ounce/410 g) cans
no salt added, diced tomatoes
with herbs

½ cup (120 ml) Homemade
Vegetable Stock (page 162)

½ small onion, 2 ounces
(56 g), halved

1 stalk celery, 2 ounces
(56 g), halved

1 small garlic clove, peeled

Dash of hot sauce

½ cup (120 m) unsweetened
almond milk

Sea salt and ground black pepper,
to taste

1. Place tomatoes, onion, celery, garlic, and hot sauce into the
   Vitamix container and secure lid.

2. Select Variable 1.

3. Switch machine to Start and slowly increase speed to Variable 10.

4. Blend for 6 minutes.

5. Reduce speed to Variable 1 and remove lid plug. Pour almond milk
   through the lid plug opening and replace lid plug.

6. Slowly increase speed to Variable 10.

7. Blend for 30 seconds. Season to taste with salt and pepper, if desired.

Nutritional Information

Amount Per Serving: Calories 60, Total Fat 0g, Saturated Fat 0g, Cholesterol 0mg,
Sodium 65mg, Total Carbohydrate 11g, Dietary Fiber 3g, Sugars 5g, Protein 2g

Vegan   **Vegetarian**   **Dairy-free**   **Gluten-free**

Vegetarian Chili

Preparation: 25 minutes plus overnight soaking | ***Processing:*** 30 seconds plus Pulsing
Cook Time: 8 hours | ***Yield:*** 8 servings

Chili:

1 pound (454 g) dried
black beans

4 cups (960 ml) water

6 whole allspice berries

1 teaspoon cumin seed

1 teaspoon coriander seed

¼ teaspoon aniseed

1 stick cinnamon

1 (28-ounce/794 g) can no
salt added crushed tomatoes

1 medium onion, 4 ½ ounces
(128 g), chopped

3 garlic cloves, peeled

¼ cup (38 g) chopped red
bell pepper

¼ cup (38 g) chopped
green bell pepper

1 teaspoon dried oregano

1 Tablespoon chili powder

¼ cup (22 g) cocoa powder

Optional Toppings:

¼ cup (25 g) sliced scallions

½ cup (64 g) sliced black olives

½ cup (8 g) chopped
fresh cilantro

Sea salt, to taste

1. Soak beans overnight in enough water to cover. Drain and rinse.

2. Place allspice, cumin seed, coriander seed, and aniseed into the Vitamix container and secure lid.

3. Select Variable 6.

4. Switch machine to Start and blend for 30 seconds.

Vegetarian Chili *continues on page 156*

continued from page 155

Vegetarian Chili

5. Place soaked beans, 4 cups (960 ml) water, ground spices, cinnamon stick, tomatoes, onion, garlic, bell peppers, oregano, chili powder, and cocoa powder into a 7-quart slow cooker. Cover and cook on High for 7 hours, or until the beans are tender.

6. Ladle soup into bowls. Top each with optional ingredients, if desired. Season to taste with sea salt, if desired.

Nutritional Information

Amount Per Serving (with optional toppings): *Calories 260, Total Fat 2g, Saturated Fat 0g, Cholesterol 0mg, Sodium 115mg, Total Carbohydrate 50g, Dietary Fiber 18g, Sugars 12g, Protein 15g*

Vegan   **Vegetarian**   **Dairy-free**   **Gluten-free**

Garden Fresh Vegetable Soup

Preparation: 10 minutes | **Processing:** 5 minutes 45 seconds
Yield: 6 ½ cups (1.5 l) (6 servings)

1 cup (240 ml) hot water

1 (14-ounce/398 g) can diced tomatoes

1 (10-ounce/284 g) package frozen spinach, thawed

½ medium cucumber, 6 ounces (175 g), halved

1 medium carrot, 3 ounces (80 g), halved

1 stalk celery, 2 ½ ounces (75 g), halved

⅓ cup (30 g) broccoli florets

1 vegetable bouillon cube

2 garlic cloves, peeled

5–6 thin slices (11 g) fresh ginger root

¼ teaspoon dried sage

¼ teaspoon ground cumin

¼ teaspoon dried basil

Dash of hot sauce

Sea salt, to taste

1. Place all ingredients into the Vitamix container in the order listed and secure lid.

2. Select Variable 1.

3. Switch machine to Start and slowly increase speed to Variable 10.

4. Blend for 5 minutes 45 seconds, using the tamper to press the ingredients into the blades.

5. Serve immediately. Season to taste with sea salt, if desired.

Nutritional Information

Amount Per Serving: *Calories 45, Total Fat 0.5g, Saturated Fat 0g, Cholesterol 0mg, Sodium 360mg, Total Carbohydrates 9g, Dietary Fiber 3g, Sugars 4g, Protein 3g*

Vegan

Vegetarian

Dairy-free

Chef's Note

To quickly thaw *spinach, remove foil cover and place on plate in microwave. Cook on High for 2 minutes.*

Thai Ginger Soup

Preparation: 15 minutes | **Processing:** 5 minutes | **Yield:** 1.0 l (4 ½ cups) (4 servings)

2 cups (480 ml) water

1 carrot, 3 ounces (85 g), halved

1 slice cabbage, 3 ounces
(85 g) (about 1 cup)

1 stalk celery, halved

1 slice green bell pepper, ¾ ounce
(20 g) (⅕ medium pepper)

1 piece zucchini, 2 ounces (60 g)
(⅓ of a medium)

1 spring onion, halved

1 thin slice lemon, unpeeled

½ garlic clove, peeled

1 piece fresh ginger root,
½ ounces (14 g), unpeeled

¼ fresh jalapeño

½ cup (70 g) unsalted,
roasted cashews

⅓ cup (6 g) fresh cilantro leaves

1 teaspoon (5 g) honey

1 vegetable stock cube

1. Place all ingredients into the Vitamix container in the order listed and secure lid.

2. Select Variable 1.

3. Switch machine to Start and slowly increase speed to Variable 10.

4. Blend for 5 minutes or until heavy steam escapes from the vented lid.

5. Serve immediately.

Nutritional Information

Amount Per Serving: *Calories 150, Total Fat 10g, Saturated Fat 2g, Cholesterol 0mg, Sodium 330mg, Total Carbohydrate 13g, Dietary Fiber 3g, Sugars 5g, Protein 5g*

Vegetarian **Dairy-free**

Tortilla Soup

Preparation: 15 minutes | **Processing:** 5 minutes 10 seconds
Yield: 2 ½ cups (600 ml) (2 servings)

Soup Base:

1 cup (240 ml) Homemade Chicken or Vegetable Stock (page 162–163)

1 Roma tomato, halved

1 medium carrot, halved

1 stalk celery, halved

1 thin slice onion

1 garlic clove, peeled

1 thin slice yellow squash

1 thin slice red bell pepper

1 thin slice cabbage

1 white mushroom

1 teaspoon taco seasoning

Dash of ground cumin

Optional Ingredients:

½ cup (70 g) cooked chicken, chunked

½ fresh jalapeño

¼ cup (30 g) sliced olives

¼ cup (50 g) unsalted canned corn, drained

1 ounce (28 g) tortilla chips

Sea salt and ground black pepper, to taste

Chef's Note

The Tortilla Soup recipe is a great go-to meal when you have an assortment of produce. You can blend ingredients into a hot, smooth purée, or for a heartier soup, add vegetables at the end of the recipe and use the Pulse switch to coarsely chop.

1. Place all Soup Base ingredients into the Vitamix container in the order listed and secure lid. Select Variable 1.

2. Switch machine to Start and slowly increase speed to Variable 10. Blend for 5 minutes.

3. If adding optional ingredients, reduce speed to Variable 1. Remove lid plug.

4. Drop chicken, jalapeños, olives, corn, and chips through the lid plug opening.

5. Blend an additional 10 seconds. Season to taste with salt and pepper, if desired.

Nutritional Information

Amount Per Serving (with optional ingredients): *Calories 200, Total Fat 6g, Saturated Fat 1.5g, Cholesterol 30mg, Sodium 260mg, Total Carbohydrate 23g, Dietary Fiber 4g, Sugars 5g, Protein 14g*

Dairy-free

Homemade Vegetable Stock

Preparation: 15 minutes | **Total Time:** 30 minutes
Yield: 8 cups (8 servings)

9 cups (2.1 l) water

1 Tablespoon whole peppercorns

2 or 3 bay leaves

1 small yellow onion cut into
quarters (no need to peel if
the onion is clean)

2 or 3 large garlic cloves,
unpeeled and smashed with
the side of a knife

1–2 sprigs fresh thyme,
or a large pinch of dried

3 dried mushrooms (optional)

1 dried chile (optional)

Chef's Note

Vegetable scraps — *such
as stems, skins, and
trimmings — make great
additions to homemade
stocks. When chopping
veggies for any reason,
consider saving the scraps
and freezing for later use
in a vegetable, beef, or
chicken stock.*

1. Fill a pot with water and begin warming over medium-high heat.

2. Add all ingredients and cover the pot loosely with the lid and bring to a boil.
   Reduce to a simmer continue cooking uncovered at least 10 minutes. The longer
   the broth cooks, the stronger its flavor.

3. As you prepare other ingredients for your soup recipe, add the scraps to your stock pot:
   carrot and onion ends, mushroom, celery, and tomato trimmings, stalks from greens, etc.
   This will help the stock reinforce the flavors of your soup. Since you won't be boiling
   this stock for an extended period, you can use strong-flavored vegetables usually
   forbidden in stocks such as cabbage, broccoli, cauliflower or turnip.

4. Strain the broth and add it to your soup pot when the recipe calls for it. Leftover broth can
   be stored refrigerated in an airtight container for up to 1 week or frozen for up to 3 months.

Nutritional Information

Amount Per Serving: *Calories 5, Total Fat 0g, Saturated Fat 0g, Cholesterol 0mg,
Sodium 10mg, Total Carbohydrate 1g, Dietary Fiber 0g, Sugars 0g, Protein 0g*

Vegan   **Vegetarian**   **Dairy-free**   **Gluten-free**

Homemade Chicken Stock

Preparation: 15 minutes | **Total Time:** 4 hours 15 minutes
Yield: 8 cups (8 servings)

Chef's Note

Store in an airtight container in the refrigerator for up to 1 week or freeze for up to 3 months.

4 pounds (1.8 kg) chicken leg quarters, cut in half

1 small carrot, peeled and cut into 2-inch (5 cm) pieces

1 small stalk celery, cut into 2-inch (5 cm) pieces

1 small onion, root end trimmed, peeled and cut into eighths

6 sprigs fresh parsley

2 sprigs fresh thyme

1 bay leaf

1 garlic clove, crushed and peeled

20 whole peppercorns

20 cups (4.8 l) water

1. Place chicken, carrot, celery, onion, parsley, thyme, bay leaf, garlic, and peppercorns in a stockpot or large Dutch oven (10-quart capacity). Add water. Bring to a boil over high heat, then reduce heat to maintain a simmer. Skim any foam and fat that rises to the surface. Simmer for 4 hours.

2. Place a colander over a large bowl and strain the stock, pressing on the solids to release as much liquid as possible.

3. If not using immediately, cool the stock quickly by placing the bowl into a larger bowl of ice water. Once at room temperature, remove from the ice water, cover loosely and refrigerate overnight.

4. Use a spoon to remove the congealed fat from the surface of the chilled stock, then store in an airtight container (or containers).

Nutritional Information

Amount Per Serving: Calories 20, Total Fat 1g, Saturated Fat 1g, Cholesterol 10mg, Sodium 15mg, Total Carbohydrate 2g, Dietary Fiber 0g, Sugars 1g, Protein 1g

Dairy-free   **Gluten-free**

Appetizers

Dips & Spreads

Appetizer Mains

Vegan

Vegetarian

Raw

Dairy-free

Gluten-free

Appetizers can be more than just the preview; they can be the feature presentation. Pair them with a salad or side dish for a light, yet satisfying meal.

Appetizers

DIPS & SPREADS / APPETIZER MAINS

Dried Apricot Chutney

Preparation: 10 minutes | ***Processing:*** Pulsing
Cook Time: 25–30 minutes
Yield: 2 cups (480 ml) (8 servings)

6 ounces (170 g) red pepper (about 1 ½ peppers), quartered and seeded

1-inch (2.5 cm) piece ginger root, peeled

1 (7-ounce/200 g) bag dried apricots (about 30 apricots)

½ cup (120 ml) water

½ cup (120 ml) distilled vinegar

⅓ cup (67 g) granulated sugar

1. Place red pepper, ginger root, and apricots into the Vitamix container in the order listed and secure lid.

2. Select Variable 5.

3. Pulse for 5 seconds, using the tamper to press the ingredients into the blades.

4. Pour into a 2-quart saucepan and add water, vinegar, and sugar. Mix well.

5. Bring to a boil over medium-high heat, stirring occasionally. Reduce heat to medium-low and simmer 15 to 20 minutes, stirring often to prevent sticking, until thickened.

6. Pour into storage containers and cool to room temperature. Cover and chill until needed.

Nutritional Information

Per ¼ Cup (60 ml) Serving: *Calories 100, Total Fat 0g, Saturated Fat 0g, Cholesterol 0mg, Sodium 0mg, Total Carbohydrate 25g, Dietary Fiber 3g, Sugars 20g, Protein 1g*

Vegan

Vegetarian

Dairy-free

Gluten-free

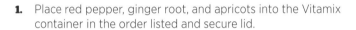

On the Menu

Chutney or Relish?

Apparently, the culinary world has yet to come to an agreement on the difference between these two condiments, but in general, relishes are made of chopped, pickled vegetables. Chutneys originated in India, and are spicy, more savory relishes that contain fruit and herbs. Chutneys are also thicker and more spreadable than relishes. Chutneys can be served as a side with hot dishes, while relishes are strictly offered as condiments.

Try this chutney recipe served atop roasted chicken or pork loin.

Cucumber Orange Relish

Preparation: 10 minutes | *Processing:* Pulsing | *Yield:* 2 cups (480 ml) (8 servings)

1 orange, peeled, halved, and seeded

¼ cup (2 g) fresh dill

1 large English cucumber, 12 ounces (340 g), cut into 2-inch (5 cm) pieces

4 teaspoons rice vinegar

½ teaspoon granulated sugar

¼ teaspoon kosher salt

1. Place orange and dill into the Vitamix container and secure lid.

2. Select Variable 5.

3. Pulse 10 to 15 times.

4. Select Variable 3.

5. Add cucumber and Pulse until coarsely chopped.

6. Place in a medium-size bowl and add vinegar, sugar, and salt. Mix well.

7. Cover and chill 2 hours or until needed. Relish should be used the same day.

Nutritional Information

Per ¼ Cup (60 g) Serving: Calories 15, Total Fat 0g, Saturated Fat 0g, Cholesterol 0mg, Sodium 60mg, Total Carbohydrate 4g, Dietary Fiber 1g, Sugars 3g, Protein 0g

 Vegan   **Vegetarian**   **Dairy-free**   **Gluten-free**

Sweet Papaya Salsa

Preparation: 20 minutes | ***Processing:*** Pulsing | ***Yield:*** 2 cups (480 ml) (16 servings)

2 Tablespoons (30 ml) fresh lime juice

1 large Roma tomato, 4 ounces (114 g), quartered

½ jalapeño, seeded

2 Tablespoons (2 g) cilantro leaves

1 shallot, 1 ounce (28 g)

14 ounces (400 g) ripe papaya (about 3 small fruits), seeded and peeled

1 garlic clove, peeled

1 teaspoon grated lime zest

½ cup (82 g) frozen corn kernels

3 Tablespoons (20 g) flaxseed meal

2 teaspoons whole flaxseed

1. Place all ingredients into the Vitamix container in the order listed and secure lid.

2. Select Variable 5.

3. Pulse 10 times, using the tamper to press the ingredients into the blades. If necessary, stop the machine and scrape down the sides of the container with a spatula. Pulse 5 more times.

Nutritional Information

Amount Per 2 Tablespoon (32 g) Serving: *Calories 25, Total Fat 0.5g, Saturated Fat 0g, Cholesterol 0mg, Sodium 0mg, Total Carbohydrate 5g, Dietary Fiber 1g, Sugars 3g, Protein 1g*

 Vegan   **Vegetarian**   **Dairy-free**   **Gluten-free**

Italian Salsa Verde

Preparation: 20 minutes | **Processing:** Pulsing plus 20 seconds
Yield: 2 ½ cups (600 ml) (20 servings)

1–2 slices fresh Italian bread

¼ cup (60 ml) red wine vinegar

2 cups (120 g) packed
parsley leaves

1 cup (240 ml) olive oil

2 Tablespoons (18 g)
capers, drained

2 Tablespoons (16 g) pine nuts

20 pitted green olives

4 anchovy filets

2 garlic cloves, peeled

2 hard-boiled egg yolks

1. Tear bread into pieces, place into the Vitamix container and secure lid.

2. Select Variable 6.

3. Pulse 5 times. Transfer bread crumbs to a sealable container.
   Measure out ⅔ cup (30 g) and place back into the Vitamix container.
   Cover and store remaining bread crumbs in a cool, dry place.

4. Add remaining ingredients to the Vitamix container in the
   order listed and secure lid.

5. Select Variable 1.

6. Switch machine to Start and slowly increase speed to Variable 7.

7. Blend for 10 seconds. Stop machine and scrape down the sides
   of the container with a spatula. Blend an additional 10 seconds or
   until desired consistency is reached.

Nutritional Information

Amount Per 2 Tablespoon (30 ml) Serving: *Calories 130, Total Fat 13g,
Saturated Fat 2g, Cholesterol 20mg, Sodium 180mg, Total Carbohydrate 2g,
Dietary Fiber 0g, Sugars 0g, Protein 1g*

Dairy-free

Verde Variations

Many cuisines from around
the world have their own
variation of a "green sauce,"
a name given to sauces that
contain mostly herbs. You may
be familiar with the classic
Mexican salsa verde, which
combines tomatillos with
jalapeños, chili peppers,
white onion, and cilantro.

In French cuisine, this sauce
is called sauce verte and
frequently refers to a type
of mayonnaise with tarragon,
parsley, and sage. Parsley is
also the green factor in Italian
Salsa Verde, which includes
capers, pine nuts, vinegar,
and anchovies.

California Salsa

Preparation: 15 minutes | ***Processing:*** Pulsing | ***Yield:*** 2 ¼ cups (540 ml) (18 servings)

½ medium onion, 2 ½ ounces (70 g), peeled and halved

1 jalapeño pepper, 1 ½ ounces (43 g), seeded

¼ cup (4 g) fresh cilantro leaves

1 teaspoon fresh lime or lemon juice

6 ripe Roma tomatoes, quartered (24 quarters)

Sea salt, to taste

1. Place onion, jalapeño, cilantro, lime, and six of the tomato quarters into the Vitamix container in the order listed and secure lid.

2. Select Variable 5.

3. Pulse 2 times.

4. Add the remaining tomato quarters through the lid plug opening. Continue to Pulse until desired consistency is reached, about 5 times.

5. Season to taste with salt. Serve with sprouted grain tortilla chips.

Nutritional Information

Amount Per 2 Tablespoon (28 g) Serving: *Calories 5, Total Fat 0g, Saturated Fat 0g, Cholesterol 0mg, Sodium 0mg, Total Carbohydrate 1g, Dietary Fiber 0g, Sugars 1g, Protein 0g*

 Vegan   **Vegetarian**   **Raw**   **Dairy-free**   **Gluten-free**

Smoky Chile Salsa

Preparation: 20 minutes | ***Processing:*** Pulsing | ***Yield:*** 1 ½ cups (360 ml) (12 servings)

¼ cup (60 ml) red wine vinegar

¼ cup (60 ml) extra virgin olive oil

2 teaspoons chipotles in adobo sauce

7 ounce (200 g) ripe tomato, quartered

2 ounce (56 g) onion wedge, peeled

1 jalapeño, halved and seeded

¼ cup (4 g) fresh cilantro leaves

Sea salt, to taste

Ground black pepper, to taste

1. Place all ingredients into the Vitamix container in the order listed and secure lid.

2. Select Variable 6.

3. Pulse 5 times. Stop machine and scrape down the sides of the container with a spatula. Secure lid and Pulse 3 more times.

4. Season to taste with salt and pepper before serving with tortilla chips or fresh vegetables.

Nutritional Information

Amount Per 2 Tablespoon (33 g) Serving: *Calories 45, Total Fat 4.5g, Saturated Fat 0.5g, Cholesterol 0mg, Sodium 5mg, Total Carbohydrate 1g, Dietary Fiber 0g, Sugars 1 g, Protein 0g*

 Vegan   **Vegetarian**   **Dairy-free**   **Gluten-free**

Hummus Dip

Preparation: 15 minutes | ***Processing:*** 30–40 seconds
Yield: 3 ¼ cups (780 ml) (26 servings)

¼ cup (60 ml) fresh lemon juice

¼ cup (60 ml) water

2 (15-ounce / 425 g) cans
no salt added chickpeas
(garbanzo beans), one
drained, one with liquid

¼ cup (35 g) raw sesame seeds

1 garlic clove, peeled

1 teaspoon ground cumin

Sea salt, to taste

1. Place all ingredients into the Vitamix container in the order listed and secure lid.

2. Select Variable 1.

3. Switch machine to Start and slowly increase speed to Variable 10.

4. Blend for 30 to 40 seconds until smooth, using the tamper to press the ingredients into the blades.

5. Season to taste with sea salt if desired.

Nutritional Information

Amount Per 2 Tablespoon (29 g) Serving: *Calories 40, Total Fat 1g, Saturated Fat 0g, Cholesterol 0mg, Sodium 10mg, Total Carbohydrate 6g, Dietary Fiber 1g, Sugars 0g, Protein 2g*

 Vegan   **Vegetarian**   **Dairy-free**   **Gluten-free**

On the Menu

A Classic Twist

With simple ingredient variations, a basic Hummus recipe can become an entirely new creation, like this Italian Hummus with tomato paste, basil, and oregano.

3 cups (720 g) canned chickpeas (garbanzo beans), drained, rinsed; ½ cup (120 ml) liquid reserved

2–3 garlic cloves, peeled

¼ cup (60 g) tahini

¼ cup (60 ml) fresh lemon juice (about 2–3 lemons)

¼ cup (60 g) tomato paste

1 Tablespoon extra virgin olive oil

2 teaspoons dried oregano

1 teaspoon dried basil

sea salt

olive slices, for garnish

1. Place all ingredients into the Vitamix container in the order listed and secure lid.

2. Select Variable 1.

3. Switch machine to Start and slowly increase speed to Variable 10.

4. Blend for 45 seconds, using the tamper to press the ingredients into the blades.

Tuscan Bean Dip

Preparation: 15 minutes | **Processing:** 20 seconds plus Pulsing
Yield: 3 cups (720 ml) (24 servings)

2 (15-ounce / 425 g) cans no salt added cannellini beans, drained, divided use

2 Tablespoons (30 ml) fresh lemon juice

¼ cup (60 ml) water

1 Tablespoon fresh oregano, or ½ teaspoon dried oregano

2 garlic cloves, peeled

½ teaspoon ground cumin

2 scallions, halved

¼ cup (28 g) sun-dried tomatoes, finely chopped, rehydrated (see instructions in margin), and drained

Several dashes of hot sauce

Sea salt, to taste

Chef's Note

To rehydrate *sun-dried tomatoes, simply place them in a bowl and cover with hot water for about 30 minutes. Using boiled water will speed up the process. Sun-dried tomatoes can also be added to hot soups or stews and will rehydrate while they cook on the stove.*

1. Place one can drained beans, lemon juice, water, oregano, garlic, and cumin into the Vitamix container in the order listed and secure lid.

2. Select Variable 1.

3. Switch machine to Start and slowly increase speed to Variable 6.

4. Blend for 20 seconds.

5. Place remaining can of beans, scallions, sun-dried tomatoes, and hot sauce into the Vitamix container in the order listed and secure lid.

6. Select Variable 6.

7. Pulse 10 times.

8. Season to taste with sea salt, if desired.

Nutritional Information

Amount Per 2 Tablespoon (42 g) Serving: *Calories 30, Total Fat 0g, Saturated Fat 0g, Cholesterol 0mg, Sodium 10mg, Total Carbohydrate 5g, Dietary Fiber 2g, Sugars 0g, Protein 2g*

Vegan   **Vegetarian**   **Dairy-free**   **Gluten-free**

Hot Wing Hummus

Preparation: 15 minutes | ***Processing:*** 45 seconds | ***Yield:*** 3 cups (720 ml) (24 servings)

3 cups (720 g) canned chickpeas (garbanzo beans), drained and rinsed; ½ cup (120 ml) liquid reserved

2–3 garlic cloves, peeled

¼ cup (60 g) tahini

¼ cup (60 ml) fresh lemon juice

1 Tablespoon white vinegar

1–2 Tablespoons barbecue sauce

3 Tablespoons (45 ml) hot sauce

1 ½ teaspoons paprika

¼ teaspoon kosher salt

1. Place all ingredients into the Vitamix container in the order listed and secure lid.

2. Select Variable 1.

3. Switch machine to Start and slowly increase speed to Variable 10.

4. Blend for 45 seconds or until smooth, using the tamper to press the ingredients into the blades. Serve with celery and carrot sticks.

Nutritional Information

Amount Per 2 Tablespoon (28 g) Serving: *Calories 45, Total Fat 2g, Saturated Fat 0g, Cholesterol 0mg, Sodium 95mg, Total Carbohydrate 6g, Dietary Fiber 0g, Sugars 0g, Protein 2g*

Vegan   **Vegetarian**   **Dairy-free**   **Gluten-free**

Lentil Hummus

Preparation: 20 minutes | **Processing:** 30–40 seconds
Cook Time: 15 minutes | **Yield:** 4 cups (960 ml) (32 servings)

½ pound (227 g) lentils,
picked over

½ cup (120 g) tahini

5 garlic cloves, peeled

¼ teaspoon salt

½ cup (120 ml) fresh
lemon juice

¾ cup (180 ml) water

½ cup (120 ml) extra
virgin olive oil

1. In a large saucepan, bring 2 quarts water with lentils to a boil and simmer about 15 minutes. Drain and rinse lentils under cold water, draining well.

2. Place lentils, tahini, garlic, salt, lemon juice, water, and oil into the Vitamix container in the order listed and secure lid.

3. Select Variable 1.

4. Switch machine to Start and slowly increase speed to Variable 10.

5. Blend for 30 to 40 seconds or until smooth, using the tamper to press the ingredients into the blades.

6. Serve with toasted pita wedges, whole-grain crackers, or fresh vegetables.

Nutritional Information

Amount Per 2 Tablespoon (30 ml) Serving: *Calories 80, Total Fat 6g, Saturated Fat 1g, Cholesterol 0mg, Sodium 20mg, Total Carbohydrate 6g, Dietary Fiber 1g, Sugars 0g, Protein 2g*

Vegan   **Vegetarian**   **Dairy-free**   **Gluten-free**

Southwest Black Bean Dip

Preparation: 15 minutes | **Processing:** 30–40 seconds
Yield: 2 cups (480 ml) (16 servings)

¼ cup (60 ml) water

1 Tablespoon balsamic vinegar

1 Tablespoon fresh lemon juice

2 Tablespoons (2 g) fresh cilantro leaves plus additional for garnish

2 garlic cloves, peeled

1 (15-ounce / 425 g) can no salt added black beans, drained, rinsed

1 teaspoon ground cumin

½ teaspoon chili powder

dash ground black pepper

1. Place all ingredients into the Vitamix container in the order listed and secure lid.

2. Select Variable 1.

3. Switch machine to Start and slowly increase speed to Variable 7.

4. Blend for 30 to 40 seconds, using the tamper to press the ingredients into the blades.

5. Garnish with chopped cilantro and serve with tortilla chips or fresh vegetables.

Nutritional Information

Amount Per 2 Tablespoon (36 g) Serving: *Calories 25, Total Fat 0g, Saturated Fat 0g, Cholesterol 0mg, Sodium 5mg, Total Carbohydrate 5g, Dietary Fiber 2g, Sugars 0g, Protein 2g*

Vegan   **Vegetarian**   **Dairy-free**   **Gluten-free**

Bright Idea

Make It A Fiesta Night

A great source of protein, Southwest Black Bean Dip can be used in a variety of dishes. For a self-serve, weeknight meal, create a build-your-own taco bar. Offer soft and crispy tortilla shells or lettuce wraps, and let everyone choose their favorite fillings, such as grilled chicken, ground beef and onion mixture, marinated tofu, and Southwest Black Bean Dip.

You could also include Taco Guac, California Salsa, and Vegan Sour Cream (also shown in this section), followed by shredded lettuce and cheeses. The best part is, all these ingredients will refrigerate well in sealed containers, so you can serve an encore performance later in the week.

Guacamole Dip

Preparation: 15 minutes | *Processing:* Pulsing | *Yield:* 2 ½ cups (600 ml) (20 servings)

1 Roma tomato, 3 ounces (85 g), quartered, divided use

4 ripe Hass avocados, halved, pitted, and peeled, divided use

½ cup (40 g) chopped red onion

2 Tablespoons (30 ml) fresh lemon or lime juice

½ cup (8 g) fresh cilantro leaves.

Sea salt, to taste

1. Place half tomato, 2 avocados, onion, lemon juice, and cilantro into the Vitamix container in the order listed and secure lid.

2. Select Variable 6.

3. Pulse until ingredients are mixed, using the tamper to press the ingredients into the blades.

4. Remove lid, add remaining avocado and tomato, and secure lid.

5. Select Variable 5.

6. Pulse 8 to 10 times until ingredients are mixed, using the tamper to press the ingredients into the blades.

7. Do not overmix. Leave chunky. Season to taste with sea salt, if desired.

Nutritional Information

Amount Per 2 Tablespoon (30 ml) Serving: Calories 50, Total Fat 4g, Saturated Fat 0.5g, Cholesterol 0mg, Sodium 0mg, Total Carbohydrate 3g, Dietary Fiber 2g, Sugars 0g, Protein 1g

 Vegan   **Vegetarian**   **Raw** **Dairy-free** **Gluten-free**

Taco Guac

Preparation: 20 minutes | ***Processing:*** 5–10 seconds | ***Yield:*** 2 ¼ cups (540 ml) (18 servings)

8 ounces (227 g) tomatillos, husked and quartered

½ cup (8 g) fresh cilantro leaves

1 ½ ounces (43 g) onion, peeled

1 ½ ounces (43 g) jalapeño, halved and seeded

1 Tablespoon fresh lime juice

2 garlic cloves, peeled

1 ripe Hass avocado, pitted and peeled

Sea salt, to taste

1. Place all ingredients into the Vitamix container in the order listed and secure lid.

2. Select Variable 1.

3. Switch machine to Start and slowly increase speed to Variable 5.

4. Blend for 5 to 10 seconds, using the tamper to press the ingredients into the blades.

5. Season to taste with sea salt, if desired.

Nutritional Information

Amount Per 2 Tablespoon (30 ml) Serving: *Calories 20, Total Fat 1.5g, Saturated Fat 0g, Cholesterol 0mg, Sodium 0mg, Total Carbohydrate 2g, Dietary Fiber 1g, Sugars 1g, Protein 0g*

 Vegan   **Vegetarian**   **Raw**   **Dairy-free** **Gluten-free**

Traditional Cheese Fondue

Preparation: 15 minutes | **Processing:** 4 minutes
Yield: 4 cups (960 ml) (32 servings)

¾ cup (180 ml) dry white wine	1 teaspoon ground black pepper
¾ cup (180 ml) water	8 ounces (227 g) Gruyere cheese, cut into 1-inch (2.5 cm) cubes
1 ½ Tablespoons Kirsch	
2 Tablespoons (16 g) cornstarch	8 ounces (227 g) Emmental cheese, cut into 1-inch (2.5 cm) cubes
¼ teaspoon ground nutmeg	

1. Place all ingredients into the Vitamix container in the order listed and secure lid.

2. Select Variable 1.

3. Switch machine to Start and slowly increase speed to Variable 10.

4. Blend for 4 minutes or until mixture is smooth and warm. Pour mixture into fondue pot.

Nutritional Information

Amount Per 2 Tablespoon (26 g) Serving: *Calories 70, Total Fat 4.5g, Saturated Fat 2.5g, Cholesterol 15mg, Sodium 50mg, Total Carbohydrate 1g, Dietary Fiber 0g, Sugars 0g, Protein 4g*

Vegetarian **Gluten-free**

Bright Idea

Revamping Leftovers

Turn weekend leftovers into weeknight dinner. Fondues are such a simple way to make a big impact when entertaining. This Traditional Cheese Fondue is a delicious precursor to any dinner spread. Offer your guests cubed country French bread, apple slices, or steamed asparagus spears, broccoli, or cauliflower. Leftover fondue can be used to make an excellent base for a soup or pasta sauce.

Substitute Swiss for Emmental cheese for a more cost-effective, yet still smooth and delicious fondue.

Chili-Cheese Fondue

Preparation: 20 minutes | *Processing:* 4 minutes | *Yield:* 3 ½ cups (840 ml) (28 servings)

¾ cup (180 ml) milk

2 Tablespoons (30 ml) tequila

1 (4-ounce/113 g) can chopped green chilies

2 garlic cloves, peeled

8 ounces (227 g) cubed Cheddar cheese

8 ounces (227 g) cubed Monterey Jack cheese

1. Place all ingredients into the Vitamix container in the order listed and secure lid.

2. Select Variable 1.

3. Switch machine to Start and slowly increase speed to Variable 10, using the tamper to press the ingredients into the blades.

4. Blend for 4 minutes until mixture is warm and cheese is melted.

Nutritional Information

Amount Per 2 Tablespoon (30 g) Serving: Calories 70, Total Fat 5g, Saturated Fat 3.5g, Cholesterol 15mg, Sodium 160mg, Total Carbohydrate 1g, Dietary Fiber 0g, Sugars 0g, Protein 5g

Vegetarian **Gluten-free**

Vegan Sour Cream

Preparation: 10 minutes plus soaking | **Processing:** 40 seconds
Yield: 2 ½ cups (600 ml) (40 servings)

Chef's Note

Substitute this Vegan Sour Cream for the dairy version in recipes that call for it as an ingredient or garnish.

2 cups (340 g) raw cashews

3 teaspoons apple cider vinegar

½ cup (120 ml) water

juice of 1 lemon plus 1 Tablespoon

Sea salt, to taste

1. Cover cashews with water and soak for a few hours or overnight.

2. Drain cashews.

3. Place cashews, vinegar, water, and lemon juice into the Vitamix container in the order listed and secure lid.

4. Select Variable 1.

5. Switch machine to Start and slowly increase speed to Variable 10.

6. Blend for 40 seconds, using the tamper to press the ingredients into the blades.

7. Season to taste with sea salt, if desired.

Nutritional Information

Amount Per 1 Tablespoon Serving: Calories 30, Total Fat 2.5g, Saturated Fat 0g, Cholesterol 0mg, Sodium 0mg, Total Carbohydrate 2g, Dietary Fiber 0g, Sugars 0g, Protein 1g

Vegan   **Vegetarian**   **Raw**   **Dairy-free**   **Gluten-free**

Aioli

Preparation: 10 minutes | ***Processing:*** 1 minute
Yield: 1 ¾ cups (420 ml) (28 servings)

3 large pasteurized egg yolks

¼ cup (60 ml) fresh lemon juice

1 teaspoon salt

⅛ teaspoon ground white pepper

3 large garlic cloves, peeled

1 ½ cups (360 ml) light olive oil

1. Place egg yolks, lemon juice, salt, pepper, and garlic into the Vitamix container in the order listed and secure lid.

2. Select Variable 1.

3. Switch machine to Start and slowly increase speed to Variable 5. Remove lid plug.

4. While machine is running, slowly pour oil through the lid plug opening. As the mixture begins to thicken, the oil may be added at a faster rate. Process should take no longer than 1 minute.

5. Refrigerate in an airtight container.

Nutritional Information

Amount Per 1 Tablespoon Serving: *Calories 110, Total Fat 12g, Saturated Fat 2g, Cholesterol 20mg, Sodium 85mg, Total Carbohydrate 0g, Dietary Fiber 0g, Sugars 0g, Protein 0g*

Vegetarian   **Dairy-free**   **Gluten-free**

Citrus Fruit Dip

Preparation: 15 minutes | **Processing:** 15 seconds
Yield: 3 ½ cups (840 ml) (28 servings)

3 cups (720 g) plain, unsweetened soy yogurt, strained to remove excess moisture

¼ cup (60 ml) honey

¼ lime, peeled

⅛ orange, peeled

½-inch (1.3 cm) square piece lime peel or 1 Tablespoon lime zest

½-inch (1.3 cm) square piece orange peel or 1 Tablespoon orange zest

1. Place all ingredients into the Vitamix container in the order listed and secure lid.

2. Select Variable 1.

3. Switch machine to Start and slowly increase speed to Variable 10.

4. Blend for 15 seconds.

5. Serve as a dip with fresh fruit or layer with granola and fruit for a delicious breakfast parfait.

Nutritional Information

Amount Per 2 Tablespoon (29 g) Serving: *Calories 25, Total Fat 0.5g, Saturated Fat 0g, Cholesterol 0mg, Sodium 0mg, Total Carbohydrate 3g, Dietary Fiber 0g, Sugars 3g, Protein 1g*

Vegetarian **Dairy-free** **Gluten-free**

Pineapple, Pepper, and Pecan Cheese Spread

Preparation: 15 minutes | **Processing:** 30 seconds plus Pulsing
Yield: 2 ¼ cups (540 ml) (18 servings)

11 ounces (312 g) cream
cheese, softened

⅛ teaspoon cayenne pepper

3 green onions, cut in 1-inch
(2.5 cm) pieces (white and
pale green parts only)

½ green bell pepper,
cut in 4 pieces

½ cup (83 g) fresh
pineapple chunks

½ cup (50 g) pecan halves

Chef's Note

Make your presentations
just as appetizing as your
dips by getting creative.
A scooped-out pineapple
half is a fun way to present
fruit dips such as the
Pineapple, Pepper and
Pecan Cheese Spread.

1. Place cheese, cayenne pepper, and green onions into the Vitamix container
    in the order listed and secure lid. Select Variable 1.

2. Switch machine to Start and blend for 20 seconds. Stop machine and remove lid.

3. Add bell pepper to the Vitamix container and secure lid. Select Variable 3.

4. Pulse 5 times. Stop machine and use a spatula to loosen food under blades.

5. Add pineapple to the Vitamix container and secure lid. Select Variable 5.

6. Pulse 3 times. Remove lid and scrape down the sides of the container with a spatula, if necessary.

7. Add nuts to the Vitamix container and secure lid. Select Variable 3.

8. Pulse 2 or 3 times.

9. Remove lid and scrape down the sides of the container with a spatula.
    Loosen any pieces caught under the blades and secure lid. Select Variable 1.

10. Switch machine to Start and blend 10 seconds.

11. Transfer to a serving bowl or covered storage container. If desired, refrigerate several hours to blend
    flavors. May be stored in the refrigerator for 1 week. Serve with crackers or fresh vegetable crudités.

Nutritional Information

Amount Per 2 Tablespoon (30 g) Serving: Calories 80, Total Fat 7g, Saturated Fat 3g,
Cholesterol 20mg, Sodium 75mg, Total Carbohydrate 2g, Dietary Fiber 0g, Sugars 2g, Protein 1g

Vegetarian **Gluten-free**

Citrus Butter

Preparation: 30 minutes | **Processing:** 30 seconds
Yield: 3 cups (720 ml) (48 servings)

1 medium orange, peeled

1 lemon, peeled with 2-inch x 1-inch
(5 cm x 2.5 cm) slice of peel remaining

1 lime, peeled with 2-inch x 1-inch
(5 cm x 2.5 cm) slice of peel remaining

8–12 sprigs fresh parsley

1 pound (454 g) salted butter, softened

1. Place all ingredients into the Vitamix container in the order listed and secure lid.

2. Select Variable 1.

3. Switch machine to Start and slowly increase speed to Variable 10.

4. Blend for 30 seconds or until smooth, using the tamper to press the ingredients into the blades.

5. Roll in plastic wrap and form a log. Freeze until ready to use.

Nutritional Information

Amount Per 1 Tablespoon Serving: *Calories 70, Total Fat 8g,
Saturated Fat 5g, Cholesterol 20mg, Sodium 70mg,
Total Carbohydrate 1g, Dietary Fiber 0g, Sugars 0g, Protein 0g*

Vegetarian **Gluten-free**

Make It Your Own

Flavored Butters

Using flavored butter is one of the quickest, easiest, and most delicious ways to transform your homemade meals from mediocre to restaurant-quality. With a little creativity, you can add an artisanal touch to the simplest of foods.

In addition to this Citrus Butter, you can also incorporate a variety of seasonal herbs such as basil, chives, rosemary, and cilantro to make a savory butter that's perfect for tossing with hot pasta and vegetables or drizzling on grilled meats.

Soft Pretzels

Preparation: 10 minutes | **Processing:** 5 seconds plus Pulsing
Bake Time: 8–10 minutes | **Yield:** 12 pretzels

¾ cup (180 ml) warm water, 105°F–115°F (40°C–46°C)

¼ cup (55 g) lightly packed brown sugar

1 package (1 Tablespoon) active dry yeast

¼ cup (30 g) whole wheat flour

½ cup (62 g) unbleached, all-purpose flour

1 ½ cups (205 g) bread (high gluten) flour

pinch salt

1 large egg mixed with 2 Tablespoons (30 ml) water (for brushing dough before baking)

Kosher salt

1. Preheat oven to 450°F (230°C).

2. To proof the yeast, combine warm water, brown sugar, and yeast. Stir quickly to combine. Set aside for 5 minutes.

3. Place flours and salt into the Vitamix container and secure lid.

4. Select Variable 1.

5. Turn machine on and slowly increase speed to Variable 2. Blend until a hole forms in the center of the flour mixture, about 5 seconds.

6. Select Variable 3. Turn machine on and remove the lid plug. Add the yeast mixture through the lid plug opening. Stop machine and replace lid plug.

7. Select Variable 10. Quickly Pulse five times. Stop machine and remove lid.

8. While dough rests, lightly coat a baking sheet with vegetable cooking spray or shortening.

9. Use a wet nylon spatula to scrape the sides of the container, pulling the dough away from the container sides and into the center of the mixture. Replace lid.

10. Select Variable 10. Quickly Pulse five times. Add additional water, 1 Tablespoon at a time, only if dough seems exceptionally dry. Repeat process three times, scraping the sides of the container until the dough binds together into a soft, elastic mixture.

Soft Pretzels continues on page 194

continued from page 193

Soft Pretzels

11. With the lid on the container, let the dough rise until doubled in size, about 15 minutes.

12. Transfer dough to a lightly floured surface and divide into 12 pieces. With your palms, roll each piece to form a rope about 12 inches to 18 inches (30 cm – 46 cm) long. Loop into an oval, twist the ends together and gently press the ends to the top side of the oval.

13. Whisk together the egg and water. Quickly and gently brush the egg mixture on each pretzel shape, and then sprinkle with kosher salt.

14. Bake for 8 to 10 minutes or until crispy and lightly browned. Best when served warm.

Nutritional Information

Amount Per Serving: *Calories 120, Total Fat 1g, Saturated Fat 0g, Cholesterol 15mg, Sodium 10mg, Total Carbohydrate 23g, Dietary Fiber 1g, Sugars 5g, Protein 4g*

Vegetarian

Dairy-free

Summer Corn Cakes

Preparation: 20 minutes | ***Processing:*** 25 seconds | ***Cook Time:*** 40 minutes | ***Yield:*** 10 cakes

½ cup (62 g) whole wheat flour

½ teaspoon baking powder

½ cup (120 ml) milk

2 large eggs

2 Tablespoons (30 ml) canola oil, divided use

½ teaspoon salt

¼ teaspoon ground black pepper

½ cup (12 g) fresh basil leaves

2 cups (308 g) fresh corn kernels (from 2 large ears)

1. Combine flour and baking powder in a medium-size mixing bowl. Set aside.

2. Place milk, eggs, 1 Tablespoon oil, salt, and pepper into the Vitamix container and secure lid. Select Variable 1.

3. Switch machine to Start and blend for 10 seconds.

4. Remove lid plug and add basil through the lid plug opening. Blend an additional 10 seconds. Stop machine and remove lid.

5. Add corn kernels to the Vitamix container and secure lid. Select Variable 1.

6. Switch machine to Start and blend 5 seconds. Pour wet mixture into dry ingredients and mix by hand to combine.

7. Heat remaining 1 Tablespoon oil in a large nonstick skillet over medium heat. Pour ¼ cup (60 ml) batter for each cake. Cook until edges are dry, about 2 minutes. Flip and cook 2 minutes more, until golden brown.

Nutritional Information

Amount Per Cake: *Calories 90, Total Fat 4.5g, Saturated Fat 1g, Cholesterol 40mg, Sodium 160mg, Total Carbohydrate 11g, Dietary Fiber 1g, Sugars 2g, Protein 3g*

Vegetarian

Crab Cakes with Sweet Chilli Dipping Sauce

Preparation: 25 minutes | **Processing:** 30 seconds plus Pulsing | **Cook Time:** 8 minutes
Chill Time: 30 minutes–2 hours | **Yield:** 4 servings

Crab Cakes:

5–6 slices of bread, torn into large pieces

1 red pepper, quartered and seeded

2 spring onions, halved

3 sprigs fresh cilantro

14 ounces (400 g) white crabmeat, divided use

3 Tablespoons (45 g) mayonnaise

1 large egg white

Zest of 1 lime

1 Tablespoon lime juice

Pinch of cayenne pepper

Dash of hot sauce

Salt, to taste

Ground black pepper, to taste

3 Tablespoons (45 ml) olive oil

Dipping Sauce:

2 medium tomatoes, quartered

4 ounces (110 g) granulated sugar

6 Tablespoons (90 ml) rice wine vinegar

2 red chilies, seeded

2 garlic cloves, peeled

1 Tablespoon lime juice

1 Tablespoon Thai fish sauce

1. Secure lid on the Vitamix machine and select Variable 3.

2. Switch machine to Start, remove lid plug, and drop bread pieces through the lid plug opening into the container, using the tamper to push them into the blades.

3. Blend 5 seconds or until bread crumbs form. Transfer to a small-size bowl and set aside.

4. Place the red pepper, spring onions, and cilantro into the Vitamix container and secure lid.

5. Select Variable 4.

Crab Cakes with Sweet Chilli Dipping Sauce continues on page 198

continued from page 197

Crab Cakes with
Sweet Chilli Dipping Sauce

6. Pulse 2 to 3 times until finely chopped, using the tamper to press the ingredients into the blades. Remove the lid and add 4 ounces (113 g) crabmeat, mayonnaise, egg white, lime zest, lime juice, cayenne pepper, hot sauce, salt, and pepper to the Vitamix container.

7. Continue to Pulse a few times until the mixture forms a coarse paste. Do not over-process.

8. Transfer to a separate large-size bowl and add remaining 10 ounces (284 g) crabmeat. Stir gently to combine. Add enough of the bread crumbs to form a stiff mixture. Put the remaining bread crumbs on a plate. Wash the Vitamix container.

9. Shape the crab mixture into 8 patties of equal size. Coat in the bread crumbs, pressing the crumbs onto each side.

10. Transfer to a clean plate, cover, and chill 30 minutes to 2 hours.

11. Place all dipping sauce ingredients into the Vitamix container in the order listed and secure lid.

12. Select Variable 1.

13. Switch machine to Start and slowly increase speed to Variable 10.

14. Blend for 20 to 25 seconds, using the tamper to press the ingredients into the blades. Transfer to a medium-size bowl and set aside.

15. Heat olive oil in a frying pan over medium-high heat. Add half of the crab cakes and fry for 2 minutes on each side until crisp and golden. Transfer to a plate and keep warm while you cook the remaining cakes. Serve warm with dipping sauce.

Nutritional Information

Per 2 Crab Cakes and 2 Tablespoons (30 ml) Sauce: *Calories 370, Total Fat 21g, Saturated Fat 3g, Cholesterol 60mg, Sodium 600mg, Total Carbohydrate 24g, Dietary Fiber 2g, Sugars 9g, Protein 21g*

Potstickers

Preparation: 20 minutes | **Processing:** Pulsing
Cook Time: 10 minutes per batch | **Yield:** 60 potstickers (15 servings)

1 ¼ pounds (567 g) Chinese, Napa, or Savoy cabbage, cut into 1 ½-inch (4 cm) chunks, divided use

1 ½ bunches green onions, washed, trimmed, and halved, divided use

8 garlic cloves, peeled, divided use

½ cup (65 g) chopped fresh ginger root, divided use

¼ cup (60 ml) soy sauce

1 Tablespoon dark sesame oil

1 teaspoon fish sauce

1 package gyoza wrappers

1 teaspoon cornstarch mixed with 1 Tablespoon cold water

1 Tablespoon canola oil

1. Place half of the cabbage, half of the green onions, half of the garlic, and half of the ginger into the Vitamix container. Add water until the ingredients float above the blades and secure lid.

2. Select Variable 10.

3. Pulse 5 times. Drain and transfer to a large-size bowl. Repeat process with remaining half of ingredients.

4. Add soy sauce, sesame oil, and fish sauce to the chopped vegetables and mix by hand until evenly combined.

5. Lay gyoza wrappers flat and fill with about 1 to 1 ½ teaspoons filling. Moisten a fingertip in the cornstarch and water mixture then rub along the edge of the dumpling. Pull bottom up and pinch together excess dumpling dough. Try to squeeze as much air out of the dumpling as you can while pinching sides. It will look like a pierogi. Press firmly together with a fork until it sticks.

6. Heat a heavy nonstick skillet with a tight-fitting lid over medium-high heat. Pour canola oil into the skillet and swirl to coat the bottom. Sauté potstickers for 3 minutes. Add ½ cup (120 ml) warm water to the pan and cover immediately. Steam covered for 5 minutes.

Nutritional Information

Amount Per Serving (4 potstickers): *Calories 90, Total Fat 1.5g, Saturated Fat 0g, Cholesterol 0mg, Sodium 480mg, Total Carbohydrate 17g, Dietary Fiber 1g, Sugars 1g, Protein 3g*

Dairy-free

Dressings & Marinades

Vegan

Vegetarian

Dairy-free

Gluten-free

Easily adjust dressings *and marinades to your own flavor profiles by changing up the herbs and spices. As chefs say, "walk through the garden" to see what you have on hand.*

Dressings & Marinades

SALAD DRESSINGS / MARINADES & RUBS

Orange Vanilla Vinaigrette

Preparation: 15 minutes | **Processing:** 30 seconds
Yield: 3 cups (720 ml) (24 servings)

2 oranges, peeled and halved

1 Tablespoon apple cider vinegar

1 ½ teaspoons vanilla extract

1 Tablespoon honey

1 lemon, peeled and halved

1 dash hot sauce

¼ teaspoon salt

⅛ teaspoon ground
black pepper

1 ½ cups (360 ml)
extra virgin olive oil

Chef's Note

Salad dressings make wonderful marinades for fish or poultry. Toss meat with dressing in a sealed plastic bag or brush on during grilling.

1. Place oranges, vinegar, vanilla, honey, lemon, hot sauce, salt, and pepper into the Vitamix container in the order listed and secure lid.

2. Select Variable 1.

3. Switch machine to Start and slowly increase speed to Variable 6.

4. Blend for 20 seconds or until smooth. Reduce speed to Variable 1 and remove the lid plug.

5. Slowly pour olive oil through the lid plug opening until emulsified.

6. Serve over spinach salad with mandarin oranges.

Nutritional Information

Amount Per 2 Tablespoon (30 ml) Serving: *Calories 140, Total Fat 14g, Saturated Fat 2g, Cholesterol 0mg, Sodium 25mg, Total Carbohydrate 2g, Dietary Fiber 0g, Sugars 2g, Protein 0g*

Vegetarian

Dairy-free

Gluten-free

Chef's Note

This dressing is perfect on a fresh spinach and mixed greens salad topped with shredded coconut and toasted almonds. For a more complex dish, serve over grilled salmon and seasonal vegetables.

Pineapple Salad Dressing

Preparation: 15 minutes | **Processing:** 35 seconds
Yield: 2 ½ cups (600 ml) (20 servings)

½ cup (120 ml) pineapple juice

4 ounces (114 g) pineapple chunks

1 lemon, peeled and halved

¼ cup (60 ml) white vinegar

2 Tablespoons (30 ml) honey

1 cup (240 ml) olive oil

1. Place juice, pineapple, lemon, vinegar, and honey into the Vitamix container in the order listed and secure lid.

2. Select Variable 1.

3. Switch machine to Start and slowly increase speed to Variable 7.

4. Blend for 15 seconds.

5. Reduce speed to Variable 3 and remove the lid plug. Slowly pour oil through the lid plug opening. Continue blending until oil is fully emulsified, about 10 seconds.

Nutritional Information

Amount Per 2 Tablespoon (30 ml) Serving: Calories 110, Total Fat 11g, Saturated Fat 1.5g, Cholesterol 0mg, Sodium 0mg, Total Carbohydrate 3g, Dietary Fiber 0g, Sugars 3g, Protein 0g

Vegetarian   **Dairy-free**   **Gluten-free**

Fresh Apple and Pear Dressing

Preparation: 15 minutes | **Processing:** 20 seconds plus Pulsing
Cook Time: 30 minutes | **Yield:** 2 ¼ cups (540 ml) (16 servings)

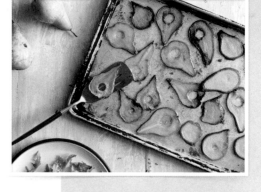

1 ripe pear, 8 ounces (227 g), cored and chopped

1 ripe apple, 8 ounces (227 g), cored and chopped

¼ cup (60 ml) honey

⅔ cup (160 ml) water

1 teaspoon fresh tarragon leaves, or 2 teaspoons dried

2 Tablespoons (30 ml) apple cider vinegar

2 Tablespoons (30 ml) fresh lemon juice

1. Place fruit, honey, water, and tarragon in a medium-size saucepan. Bring to a simmer, covered over medium heat. Remove lid and cook until very soft, about 8 minutes.

2. Continue to simmer and let water evaporate. There should be about 1 ¾ cups (420 ml) fruit and liquid when finished cooking. Allow the mixture to cool 15 minutes.

3. Pour mixture into the Vitamix container and secure lid. Select Variable 1.

4. Switch machine to Start and slowly increase speed to Variable 10.

5. Blend for 20 seconds or until smooth.

6. Add apple cider vinegar and lemon juice to the Vitamix container and secure lid. Select Variable 2.

7. Pulse 2 to 3 times to combine. Refrigerate until cooled.

Nutritional Information

Amount Per 2 Tablespoon (30 ml) Serving: *Calories 30, Total Fat 0g, Saturated Fat 0g, Cholesterol 0mg, Sodium 0mg, Total Carbohydrate 8g, Dietary Fiber 1g, Sugars 6g, Protein 0g*

Vegetarian   **Dairy-free**   **Gluten-free**

Bright Idea

Roasting Pears

To bring out a deeper flavor in the pears, try roasting them. Preheat the oven to 425°F. Peel, core, and slice the pears. Toss them in a bit of lemon juice (to prevent browning). Bake in a single layer for 25–30 minutes until tender and golden-brown.

Roasted pears also make a great topping for salads. And for those of you with a sweet tooth, try roasting the pears with a little brown sugar sprinkled on top and serve with vanilla ice cream.

Raspberry Vinaigrette

Preparation: 10 minutes | ***Processing:*** 20–30 seconds | ***Yield:*** 1 ¾ cups (420 ml) (14 servings)

¾ cup (180 ml) olive oil

¼ cup (60 ml) apple cider or raspberry vinegar

1 teaspoon salt

1 teaspoon dried basil

½ cup (60 g) fresh or frozen unsweetened
red raspberries

¼ cup (60 ml) water

2 Tablespoons (30 ml) honey

1. Place olive oil, vinegar, salt, basil, raspberries, and water into the
   Vitamix container in the order listed and secure lid.

2. Select Variable 1.

3. Switch machine to Start and remove lid plug. Add honey through the lid
   plug opening and replace lid plug.

4. Slowly increase speed to Variable 6.

5. Blend for 20 to 30 seconds. Serve immediately or refrigerate
   for up to 2 weeks.

Nutritional Information

Amount Per 2 Tablespoon (30 ml) Serving: *Calories 120, Total Fat 12g, Saturated Fat 1.5g,
Cholesterol 0mg, Sodium 170mg, Total Carbohydrate 4g, Dietary Fiber 0g, Sugars 2g, Protein 0g*

Vegetarian **Dairy-free** **Gluten-free**

Carrot Ginger Vinaigrette

Preparation: 15 minutes | **Processing:** 20 seconds | **Cook Time:** 15 minutes
Yield: 1 ½ cups (360 ml) (12 servings)

4 ounces (114 g) carrot,
rough chopped

1 cup (240 ml) water

¼ cup (60 ml) rice vinegar

2 teaspoons fresh lemon juice

4 teaspoons low-sodium
soy sauce

4 teaspoons sesame oil

¼ teaspoon salt

2 teaspoons packed light
brown sugar

2 Tablespoons (12 g)
chopped fresh ginger root

1. Place carrot and water in a small saucepan. Bring to a simmer over medium-low
   heat and cook until tender, about 15 minutes. Reserve ½ cup (120 ml) cooking
   liquid, and drain the carrots.

2. Place carrots, cooking liquid, vinegar, lemon juice, soy sauce, sesame oil, salt,
   brown sugar, and ginger into the Vitamix container in the order listed and secure lid.

3. Select Variable 1.

4. Switch machine to Start and slowly increase speed to Variable 7.

5. Blend for 20 seconds. Chill thoroughly before serving.

Nutritional Information

Amount Per 2 Tablespoon (30 ml) Serving: *Calories 25, Total Fat 1.5g, Saturated Fat 0g,
Cholesterol 0mg, Sodium 180mg, Total Carbohydrate 3g, Dietary Fiber 0g, Sugars 3g, Protein 0g*

Vegan   **Vegetarian**   **Dairy-free**

Parmesan Balsamic Vinaigrette

Preparation: 10 minutes | **Processing:** 30 seconds | **Yield:** 1 ½ cups (360 ml) (12 servings)

¼ cup (60 ml)
balsamic vinegar

1 lemon, peeled

1 small garlic clove, peeled

½ teaspoon salt

3 Tablespoons (4 g)
fresh basil leaves

3 Tablespoons (4 g)
fresh thyme leaves

½ cup (40 g) finely
grated Parmesan cheese

¼ teaspoon ground
black pepper

1 cup (240 ml) extra virgin
olive oil, divided use

1. Place balsamic vinegar, lemon, garlic, salt, fresh herbs, Parmesan, pepper, and ½ cup (120 ml) olive oil into the Vitamix container in the order listed and secure lid.

2. Select Variable 1.

3. Turn machine on and slowly increase speed to Variable 6.

4. Blend for 5 seconds. Reduce speed to Variable 1 and remove lid plug.

5. Pour remaining ½ cup (120 ml) oil through the lid plug opening in a slow, steady stream and replace lid plug.

6. Slowly increase speed to Variable 8.

7. Blend for an additional 15 seconds or until emulsified.

Nutritional Information

Amount Per 2 Tablespoon (30 ml) Serving: Calories 190, Total Fat 20g, Saturated Fat 3g, Cholesterol 5mg, Sodium 150mg, Total Carbohydrate 2g, Dietary Fiber 0g, Sugars 1g, Protein 1g

Vegetarian **Gluten-free**

Caesar Salad Dressing

Preparation: 15 minutes | ***Processing:*** 45 seconds
Yield: 4 cups (960 ml) (32 servings)

6 large eggs

2 Tablespoons (30 ml) red
wine vinegar

½ cup (120 ml) plus
1 Tablespoon fresh lemon juice

1 ½ small garlic cloves, peeled

1 cup (100 g) grated
Parmesan cheese

½ teaspoon salt

1 Tablespoon plus
1 ½ teaspoons anchovy filets

⅓ teaspoon dry mustard

1 cup (240 ml) plus
2 Tablespoons (30 ml)
extra virgin olive oil

1. Place eggs, vinegar, lemon juice, garlic, cheese, salt, anchovy, and
   mustard into the Vitamix container in the order listed and secure lid.

2. Select Variable 1.

3. Switch machine to Start and slowly increase speed to Variable 7.

4. Blend for 25 seconds or until smooth. Reduce speed to Variable 2 and remove lid plug.

5. Slowly pour olive oil through the lid plug opening and blend an additional 10 seconds.

Nutritional Information

Amount Per 2 Tablespoon (30 ml) Serving: *Calories 100, Total Fat 10g, Saturated Fat 2g,
Cholesterol 40mg, Sodium 115mg, Total Carbohydrate 1g, Dietary Fiber 0g, Sugars 0g, Protein 2g*

Gluten-free

Raspberry Maple Dressing

Preparation: 10 minutes | **Processing:** 20 seconds
Yield: 2 ½ cups (600 ml) (20 servings)

1 cup (240 ml) raspberry vinegar (see sidebar)

¼ cup (60 ml) maple syrup

Pinch of salt

Pinch of ground black pepper

1 ¼ cups (300 ml) olive oil

1. Place vinegar, maple syrup, salt, and pepper into the Vitamix container in the order listed and secure lid.

2. Select Variable 1.

3. Switch machine to Start and slowly increase speed to Variable 7.

4. Remove lid plug and slowly pour olive oil through the lid plug opening.

5. Once all the oil is incorporated, slowly increase speed to Variable 10 and continue blending for 10 seconds.

Nutritional Information

Amount Per 2 Tablespoon (30 ml) Serving: *Calories 140, Total Fat 14g, Saturated Fat 2g, Cholesterol 0mg, Sodium 0mg, Total Carbohydrate 4g, Dietary Fiber 0g, Sugars 3g, Protein 0g*

 Vegan   **Vegetarian**   **Dairy-free**   **Gluten-free**

Create Your Own

Homemade Vinegars

Here's a simple way to create colorful, healthy, delicious vinegars perfect for any gift-giving occasion.

Fill a pint jar with freshly washed red raspberries, packing the raspberries to fill the jar. Pour apple cider vinegar over the raspberries, being sure to cover them completely. Cover the jar securely with plastic wrap and place on a sunny windowsill for 4 to 6 weeks.

Strain the liquid through cheesecloth or a very fine mesh strainer; discard the raspberries. Pour raspberry vinegar into a decorative bottle and store in a cool, dry cabinet. Friends and relatives will enjoy tossing this light raspberry vinegar with a salmon salad, using it as a marinade, or incorporating it into other recipes.

Basic Vinaigrette

Preparation: 10 minutes | **Processing:** 30 seconds
Yield: 2 ¼ cups (540 ml) (18 servings)

½ cup (120 ml) red wine vinegar

2 teaspoons Dijon-style mustard

½ teaspoon ground black pepper

½–1 teaspoon kosher salt

1 ½ cups (360 ml) olive oil

½ cup (10 g) fresh herb blend (see note)

1. Place vinegar, mustard, pepper, and salt into the Vitamix container in the order listed and secure lid.

2. Select Variable 1.

3. Switch machine to Start and slowly increase speed to Variable 3.

4. Blend for 10 seconds. Remove the lid plug and slowly drizzle oil through the lid plug opening. Once oil is incorporated, add the herbs through the lid plug opening and blend for 10 seconds.

Nutritional Information

Amount Per 2 Tablespoon (30 ml) Serving: *Calories 160, Total Fat 18g, Saturated Fat 2.5g, Cholesterol 0mg, Sodium 70mg, Total Carbohydrate 0g, Dietary Fiber 0g, Sugars 0g, Protein 0g*

Vegan   **Vegetarian**   **Dairy-free**   **Gluten-free**

Chef's Note

Try oregano, *sage, and dill for a fresh herb blend, but any blend will work. Refrigerate in an airtight container for up to 2 weeks.*

Light Ranch Dressing

Preparation: 15 minutes | **Processing:** 15–20 seconds
Yield: 2 ¼ cups (540 ml) (18 servings)

1 ⅓ cups (320 ml)
low-fat buttermilk

½ cup (120 g)
light mayonnaise

4 teaspoons
Worcestershire sauce

1 teaspoon onion powder

1 teaspoon dried onion flakes

½ teaspoon garlic powder

2 Tablespoons (6 g)
fresh chives

2 Tablespoons (1 g)
fresh dill

2 Tablespoons (8 g)
fresh parsley leaves

1. Place all ingredients into the Vitamix container in the order listed and secure lid.

2. Select Variable 1.

3. Switch machine to Start and slowly increase speed to Variable 6.

4. Blend for 15 to 20 seconds.

Nutritional Information

Amount Per 2 Tablespoon (30 ml) Serving: *Calories 30, Total Fat 2.5g, Saturated Fat 0g, Cholesterol 5mg, Sodium 75mg, Total Carbohydrate 2g, Dietary Fiber 0g, Sugars 1g, Protein 1g*

Gluten-free

Light Italian Dressing

Preparation: 15 minutes | ***Processing:*** 20 seconds | ***Yield:*** 1 ½ cups (360 ml) (12 servings)

1 medium tomato, 3 ½ ounces (99 g), halved

2 Tablespoons (30 ml) red wine vinegar

2 Tablespoons (30 ml) fresh lemon juice

½ cup (120 ml) water

4 teaspoons Dijon-style mustard

⅛ teaspoon granulated sugar

2 Tablespoons (30 ml) extra virgin olive oil

1 garlic clove, peeled

¼ teaspoon dried oregano

¼ teaspoon dried basil

⅛ teaspoon kosher salt

Ground black pepper, to taste

1. Place all ingredients into the Vitamix container in the order listed and secure lid.

2. Select Variable 1.

3. Switch machine to Start and slowly increase speed to Variable 6.

4. Blend for 20 seconds. Serve immediately or refrigerate in an airtight container for up to 2 weeks.

Nutritional Information

Amount Per 2 Tablespoon (30 ml) Serving: *Calories 25, Total Fat 2.5g, Saturated Fat 0g, Cholesterol 0mg, Sodium 60mg, Total Carbohydrate 1g, Dietary Fiber 0g, Sugars 0g, Protein 0g*

 Vegan
 Vegetarian
 Dairy-free
 Gluten-free

Chef's Note

This is a great accompaniment to beef, pork, chicken, and tofu as a marinade, or brush on protein before grilling.

Citrus Honey Marinade

Preparation: 25 minutes | **Processing:** 20 seconds
Yield: 1 cup (240 ml) (8 servings)

¾ cup (180 ml) pineapple juice

2 Tablespoons (30 ml) honey

1 Tablespoon fresh lime juice

1 teaspoon lime zest

2 garlic cloves, peeled

½ teaspoon cumin seeds

2 teaspoons chopped cilantro leaves

½ jalapeño, ½ ounce (14 g), seeded

1. Place all ingredients into the Vitamix container in the order listed and secure lid.

2. Select Variable 1.

3. Switch machine to Start and slowly increase speed to Variable 7.

4. Blend for 20 seconds.

Nutritional Information

Amount Per 2 Tablespoon (30 ml) Serving: *Calories 30, Total Fat 0g, Saturated Fat 0g, Cholesterol 0mg, Sodium 0mg, Total Carbohydrate 8g, Dietary Fiber 0g, Sugars 6g, Protein 0g*

Vegetarian   **Dairy-free**   **Gluten-free**

Fresh Ginger Peanut Teriyaki Marinade

Preparation: 15 minutes | **Processing:** 20–30 seconds | **Yield:** 3 cups (720 ml) (24 servings)

¾ cup (180 ml) soy sauce

¼ cup (60 ml) rice vinegar

1 Tablespoon sesame oil

1 medium orange, peeled, halved, and seeded

½ lime, peeled

1 Tablespoon honey

¼ cup (40 g) fresh pineapple, core included or canned pineapple

1 garlic clove, peeled

1 teaspoon chopped fresh ginger root

¼ cup (55 g) firmly packed brown sugar

1 cup (145 g) peanuts, or ½ cup (130 g) Homemade Peanut Butter (page 106)

1. Place all ingredients into the Vitamix container in the order listed and secure lid.

2. Select Variable 1.

3. Switch machine to Start and slowly increase speed to Variable 10.

4. Blend for 20 to 30 seconds, using the tamper to press the ingredients into the blades.

Nutritional Information

Amount Per 2 Tablespoon (30 ml) Serving: Calories 60, Total Fat 3.5g, Saturated Fat 0.5g, Cholesterol 0mg, Sodium 600mg, Total Carbohydrate 6g, Dietary Fiber 1g, Sugars 4g, Protein 2g

Vegetarian   **Dairy-free**

Fajita Marinade

Preparation: 10 minutes | ***Processing:*** 30 seconds
Yield: 2 cups (480 ml) (16 servings)

½ cup (120 ml) olive oil

¼ cup (60 ml) red wine vinegar

½ cup (120 ml)
Worcestershire sauce

½ cup (120 ml) soy sauce

2 limes, peeled, halved

¼ teaspoon dried oregano

¼ teaspoon hot sauce

2 garlic cloves, peeled

1. Place all ingredients into the Vitamix container in the order listed and secure lid.

2. Select Variable 1.

3. Switch machine to Start and slowly increase speed to Variable 7.

4. Blend for 30 seconds.

Nutritional Information

Amount Per 2 Tablespoon (30 ml) Serving: *Calories 80, Total Fat 7g, Saturated Fat 1g, Cholesterol 0mg, Sodium 670mg, Total Carbohydrate 3g, Dietary Fiber 0g, Sugars 1g, Protein 1g*

Dairy-free

Kitchen Prep

Marinating 101

Besides tenderizing meat and adding flavor, another benefit of marinades is they can be made ahead of time. Marinades can be stored in the refrigerator up to 2 days if they contain fresh produce, or up to a month if they do not. Most marinades can be frozen for up to 2 months.

Always marinate in the refrigerator. Marinate beef, veal, pork, and lamb in roast, steak, or chop form for up to 2 days. Marinate poultry and cubed meat from 2 hours up to overnight, if the marinade is only mildly acidic. If you're cooking with seafood, marinate for 15 minutes to an hour.

Another handy way to save time: freeze meat in a container with a marinade. The day before you plan to cook it, move the covered container from the freezer to the refrigerator. As it thaws, the meat will absorb the marinade.

Tandoori Marinade

Preparation: 10 minutes | **Processing:** 30 seconds | **Yield:** 2 cups (480 ml) (16 servings)

2 cups (490 g) plain low-fat yogurt

⅛ teaspoon ground allspice

⅛ teaspoon ground cardamom

⅛ teaspoon ground cinnamon

⅛ teaspoon ground cloves

⅛ teaspoon ground turmeric

1. Place all ingredients into the Vitamix container in the order
   listed and secure lid.

2. Select Variable 1.

3. Switch machine to Start and slowly increase speed to Variable 3.

4. Blend for 30 seconds or until smooth.

Nutritional Information

Amount Per 2 Tablespoon (30 ml) Serving: Calories 20, Total Fat 0g, Saturated Fat 0g,
Cholesterol 0mg, Sodium 20mg, Total Carbohydrate 2g, Dietary Fiber 0g, Sugars 2g, Protein 2g

Vegetarian **Gluten-free**

Jerk Seasoning

Preparation: 10 minutes | **Processing:** 15 seconds
Yield: ¾ cup (180 ml) (36 servings)

3 Tablespoons (30 g) whole allspice berries

1 Tablespoon whole black peppercorns

2 teaspoons whole cloves

2 teaspoons crushed red pepper flakes

1 Tablespoon dried thyme leaves

1 Tablespoon kosher salt

1 teaspoon ground cinnamon

¼ cup (55 g) firmly packed brown sugar

Chef's Note

Brush strip steak with olive oil, and rub both sides with Jerk Seasoning or Spanish Spice Rub. Grill 3 to 4 minutes over high heat on each side for medium rare doneness.

1. Place allspice, peppercorns, cloves, and pepper flakes into the Vitamix container and secure lid.

2. Select Variable 1.

3. Switch machine to Start and slowly increase speed to Variable 4.

4. Blend for 10 seconds or until mixture is a medium-fine powder. Add thyme, salt, cinnamon, and brown sugar and secure lid.

5. Select Variable 1.

6. Switch machine to Start and slowly increase speed to Variable 3.

7. Blend for 5 seconds.

8. Store in covered container at room temperature. Use as a rub on grilled pork, shrimp or chicken, or any Jamaican-influenced recipe.

Nutritional Information

Amount Per 1 teaspoon Serving: *Calories 5, Total Fat 0g, Saturated Fat 0g, Cholesterol 0mg, Sodium 190mg, Total Carbohydrate 2g, Dietary Fiber 0g, Sugars 2g, Protein 0g*

Vegan   **Vegetarian**   **Dairy-free**   **Gluten-free**

Spanish Spice Rub

Preparation: 10 minutes | **Processing:** 15 seconds | **Yield:** ½ cup (120 ml) (24 servings)

6 Tablespoons (41 g) Spanish paprika

1 Tablespoon cumin seeds

1 Tablespoon fennel seeds

2 teaspoons kosher salt

1 teaspoon whole black peppercorns

1. Place all ingredients into the Vitamix container and secure lid.

2. Select Variable 1.

3. Switch machine to Start and slowly increase speed to Variable 7.

4. Blend for 15 seconds.

Nutritional Information

Amount Per 1 teaspoon Serving: *Calories 5, Total Fat 0g, Saturated Fat 0g, Cholesterol 0mg, Sodium 160mg, Total Carbohydrate 1g, Dietary Fiber 1g, Sugars 0g, Protein 0g*

Vegan   **Vegetarian**   **Dairy-free**   **Gluten-free**

Coffee Dry Rub

Preparation: 15 minutes | **Processing:** 45 seconds
Yield: ½ cup (120 ml) (24 servings)

1 ½ teaspoons sea salt

4 teaspoons ground coffee, or 1 Tablespoon whole coffee beans

1 dried Pasilla chili, seeded

2 Tablespoons (28 g) dark brown sugar

½ teaspoon ground black pepper, or ¼ teaspoon whole black peppercorns

½ teaspoon onion powder

½ teaspoon garlic powder

¼ teaspoon cayenne pepper

¼ teaspoon whole coriander seeds

¼ teaspoon ground turmeric

1. Place all ingredients into the Vitamix container in the order listed and secure lid.

2. Select Variable 1.

3. Switch machine to Start and slowly increase speed to Variable 10.

4. Blend for 45 seconds. Use immediately or store in an airtight container with your spices until ready to use.

Nutritional Information

Amount Per 1 teaspoon Serving: *Calories 5, Total Fat 0g, Saturated Fat 0g, Cholesterol 0mg, Sodium 150mg, Total Carbohydrate 1g, Dietary Fiber 0g, Sugars 1g, Protein 0g*

 Vegan   **Vegetarian**   **Dairy-free**   **Gluten-free**

Make It Your Own

Flavoring Dry Rubs

When creating homemade dry rubs, you may not think of coffee as a go-to ingredient. But combining ground coffee with certain spices results in a rich, earthy flavor that makes a great dry rub for beef, pork, and even poultry.

Control the flavor of your dry rub by adjusting spices such as turmeric, garlic powder, and coriander. You can play up the sweetness of the rub by adding brown sugar and reducing the amount of cayenne. You may even find your new favorite dry rub by experimenting with spices you have on hand. Try adding paprika, dry mustard, or ginger for a unique flavor profile.

Side Dishes

Salads & Coleslaws

Sides

Vegan

Vegetarian

Dairy-free

Gluten-free

From roasted vegetables to smooth purées, these side dishes perfectly complement almost any meal. Discover just how easy it is to prepare a side with fresh, all-natural ingredients.

Side Dishes

SALADS & COLESLAWS / SIDES

Quinoa Mango Salad

Preparation: 20 minutes | ***Processing:*** 20–30 seconds | ***Cook Time:*** 15 minutes
Yield: 10 cups (2.8 kg) salad (10 servings)

1 cup (170 g) uncooked
quinoa, rinsed

4 cups (748 g) frozen unsweetened
mango chunks, partially thawed
and drained, divided use

1 cup (145 g) golden raisins

½ cup (50 g) sliced celery (1 stalk)

¼ cup (40 g) diced red onion

½ cup (46 g) sliced
almonds, toasted

½ cup (120 g) Vegan Sour
Cream (page 186)

2 Tablespoons (30 ml)
white balsamic vinegar

2 teaspoons curry powder

1 teaspoon garlic powder

1 teaspoon ground
black pepper

1. Rinse quinoa in cool water before using. Heat 2 cups (480 ml) of water to a boil.
   Stir in quinoa and return to boil. Cover and reduce heat to simmer. Cook for 12 minutes
   or until quinoa absorbs almost all of the water. Fluff with a fork and let cool for 15 minutes.

2. Combine quinoa, 2 cups (374 g) mango, raisins, celery, red onion, and sliced
   almonds in a large bowl. Set aside.

3. Place remaining 2 cups (374 g) mango, sour cream, vinegar, curry, garlic powder, and black
   pepper into the Vitamix container in the order listed and secure lid.

4. Select Variable 1.

5. Switch machine to Start and slowly increase speed to Variable 7.

6. Blend for 20 to 30 seconds.

7. Pour dressing over quinoa mixture to taste and toss to blend. Store extra dressing
   refrigerated in an airtight container.

Nutritional Information

Amount Per Serving: *Calories 270, Total Fat 9g, Saturated Fat 1.5g, Cholesterol 0mg,
Sodium 15mg, Total Carbohydrate 43g, Dietary Fiber 5g, Sugars 25g, Protein 7g*

Vegan **Vegetarian** **Dairy-free** **Gluten-free**

Curried Vegetable Salad

Preparation: 20 minutes | **Processing:** Pulsing plus 20–30 seconds
Yield: 4 servings

1 small carrot, 2 ounces (56 g),
cut into 3 pieces

1 stalk celery, 2 ounces (56 g),
cut into 3 pieces

1 medium red bell pepper,
9 ounces (255 g), seeded
and quartered

1 medium green bell pepper,
7 ounces (200 g), seeded
and quartered

1 scallion, diced

12 ounce (340 g) English
cucumber, medium diced

6 Tablespoons (90 ml)
apple cider vinegar

½ cup (120 ml) olive oil

2 teaspoons Dijon-style mustard

2 teaspoons fresh lemon juice

1 ounce (28 g) slice red onion

½ teaspoon chopped garlic

2 teaspoons curry powder

1 teaspoon granulated sugar

⅛ teaspoon salt

1. Place carrots and celery into the Vitamix container and secure lid. Select Variable 6.
   Pulse 7 or 8 times to chop. Remove to a large bowl.

2. Place peppers into the Vitamix container and secure lid. Select Variable 5.

3. Pulse 3 times. Stop machine and remove lid. Scrape down the sides of the container with a spatula.
   Secure lid and Pulse 2 more times. Add to carrot and celery mixture. Add chopped cucumber
   and scallions to bowl and set aside.

4. Place vinegar, olive oil, mustard, lemon juice, onion, garlic, curry, sugar, and salt into the
   Vitamix container in the order listed and secure lid. Select Variable 1.

5. Switch machine to Start and slowly increase speed to Variable 10. Blend for 20 to 30 seconds.

6. Before pouring dressing over salad, drain any extra liquid from chopped vegetables.
   Toss with salad dressing and serve.

Nutritional Information

Amount Per Serving: *Calories 310, Total Fat 28g, Saturated Fat 4g, Cholesterol 0mg,
Sodium 180mg, Total Carbohydrate 14g, Dietary Fiber 4g, Sugars 8g, Protein 2g*

Vegan **Vegetarian** **Dairy-free** **Gluten-free**

Green Coleslaw

Preparation: 15 minutes | **Processing:** Pulsing | **Cook Time:** 5 minutes
Chill Time: 4 hours – overnight | **Yield:** 6 servings

½ pound (227 g) collard greens, tough stems removed, each leaf cut into quarters

1 large bell pepper, 9 ounces (256 g), any color, quartered

1 medium onion, 5 ounces (142 g), quartered

3 medium carrots, 9 ½ ounces (270 g), cut into thirds

½ cup (120 ml) apple cider vinegar

⅓ cup (67 g) granulated sugar

¼ cup (60 ml) canola oil

1 teaspoon dry mustard

1 teaspoon celery seed

½ teaspoon salt

¼ teaspoon ground black pepper

1. Place half of the collard leaves into the Vitamix container, fill to 6-cup (1.4 l) mark with water and secure lid. Select Variable 5.

2. Pulse 3 times until chopped. Strain through a colander and place in large-size mixing bowl. Repeat with remaining collard leaves.

3. Place pepper and onion quarters into the Vitamix container and secure lid. Select Variable 5.

4. Pulse 6 to 7 times until chopped. Transfer to bowl with chopped collards.

5. Place carrots into the Vitamix container and secure lid. Select Variable 6. Pulse 5 to 6 times until chopped. Add to other vegetables in bowl.

6. Add vinegar, sugar, oil, dry mustard, celery seed, salt, and pepper to a small saucepan and stir together. Bring to a boil, stirring to dissolve sugar. Remove from heat and pour over collard and vegetable mixture. Stir to coat. For best results, cover and chill 4 hours or overnight before serving.

Nutritional Information

Amount Per Serving: *Calories 170, Total Fat 10g, Saturated Fat 0.5g, Cholesterol 0mg, Sodium 240mg, Total Carbohydrate 22g, Dietary Fiber 4g, Sugars 13g, Protein 2g*

Vegan **Vegetarian** **Dairy-free** **Gluten-free**

Trimming Collard Greens

To prepare collard greens, lay each leaf flat on a cutting board. Use a sharp paring knife to cut along either side of the center spine, separating the entire leaf from the spine.

To save time, you can also fold the leaf in half, so only one cut is necessary along the spine. If children are helping out in the kitchen, have them simply pull leaves away from the stem with their hands — a less precise, but certainly practical technique.

Fresh Slaw with Fennel Seed Dressing

Preparation: 25 minutes | ***Processing:*** Pulsing plus 30–45 seconds | ***Chill Time:*** 4 hours–overnight
Yield: 10 ¼ cups (2.4 kg) (10 servings)

1 ½-pound (680 g) head green cabbage, cored, cut into 1 ½-inch (4 cm) chunks, divided use

9-ounce (256 g) fennel bulb, quartered

1 large red bell pepper, 9 ounces (256 g), quartered

4 ½ ounces (128 g) carrot, cut into thirds

1 large Granny Smith apple, 7 ½ ounces (213 g), small diced

⅔ cup (160 ml) white wine vinegar

¼ cup (50 g) granulated sugar

2 ¼ teaspoons fennel seeds

½ cup (120 g) light mayonnaise

¼ cup (60 g) reduced-fat sour cream

⅓ cup (80 ml) extra virgin olive oil

1. Place half of the cabbage into the Vitamix container, fill with water to the 6-cup (1.4 l) level and secure lid.

2. Select Variable 6.

3. Pulse 5 times. Drain and place in a large-size mixing bowl. Repeat with remaining cabbage.

4. Place fennel into the Vitamix container, fill with water to the 6-cup (1.4 l) level and secure lid.

5. Select Variable 6.

6. Pulse 5 times. Drain and add to chopped cabbage.

7. Place red pepper quarters into the Vitamix container and secure lid.

8. Select Variable 4.

9. Pulse 5 to 6 times. Transfer to bowl with other vegetables.

10. Repeat process with carrot chunks and add to bowl. Add chopped apple to the vegetable mixture.

Fresh Slaw with Fennel Seed Dressing *continues on page 232*

continued from page 231

Fresh Slaw with Fennel Seed Dressing

11. Place vinegar, sugar, and fennel seeds into the Vitamix container and secure lid.

12. Select Variable 1.

13. Switch machine to Start and slowly increase speed to Variable 10.

14. Blend for 30 to 45 seconds. Stop machine and remove lid. Add mayo, sour cream, and oil to the container and secure lid.

15. Select Variable 5.

16. Pulse 5 times until blended. Pour over chopped vegetables and toss to mix.

17. Cover and refrigerate at least 4 hours or overnight before serving.

Nutritional Information

Amount Per Serving: *Calories 190, Total Fat 12g, Saturated Fat 2g, Cholesterol 5mg, Sodium 120mg, Total Carbohydrate 18g, Dietary Fiber 4g, Sugars 12 g, Protein 2g*

Vegetarian   **Gluten-free**

Hawaiian Style Coleslaw

Preparation: 20 minutes | **Processing:** Pulsing plus 10 seconds
Yield: 9 ¾ cups (2.3 kg) (19 servings)

2 pounds (908 g) cabbage, cut into 1 ½-inch (4 cm) wedges

1 cup (165 g) fresh pineapple, cut into bite-size pieces

1 cup (189 g) canned mandarin oranges segments, drained

¾ cup (101 g) blue cheese crumbles

1 ½ cups (360 g) light mayonnaise

½ cup (100 g) chopped scallions

2 ½ Tablespoons (38 ml) fresh lemon juice

¼ teaspoon ground black pepper, plus additional, to taste

Sea salt, to taste

1. Place half of the cabbage wedges into the Vitamix container, fill with water to the 6-cup (1.4 l) mark and secure lid. Select Variable 6.

2. Pulse 5 to 6 times until chopped. Drain, remove to a large-size mixing bowl, and repeat with remaining cabbage.

3. Add pineapple, mandarin orange segments, and blue cheese to the cabbage.

4. Place the mayonnaise, scallions, lemon juice, and black pepper into the Vitamix container and secure lid. Select Variable 1.

5. Switch machine to Start and slowly increase speed to Variable 2.

6. Blend for 10 seconds.

7. Pour over vegetables and toss to combine. Season to taste with sea salt and black pepper if desired.

Nutritional Information

Amount Per ½ Cup (120 g) Serving: *Calories 110, Total Fat 8g, Saturated Fat 2g, Cholesterol 15mg, Sodium 220mg, Total Carbohydrate 7g, Dietary Fiber 2g, Sugars 4g, Protein 2g*

Vegetarian **Gluten-free**

On the Menu

Hawaiian Luau

Turn your next backyard barbeque into an island getaway. This coleslaw recipe makes almost 20 servings in a single blend, so it's an easy recipe when entertaining a large crowd. Make it the day before to save even more time.

Serve alongside grilled chicken or shrimp kabobs with green, red, and yellow bell peppers, fresh pineapple chunks, and onion. Piña Colada Cocktails (See Cocktails) and Tropical Milkshakes (See Desserts) complete the meal.

Chef's Note

To get a deeper *flavor from the pecans, toast them over medium heat in a dry skillet. Toss or stir frequently to prevent burning. Toast just until fragrant and remove from heat.*

Cranberry Pecan Salad

Preparation: 15 minutes | **Processing:** 20 seconds
Yield: 4 servings

1 cup (240 ml) cranberry juice

1 Tablespoon plus 1 ½ teaspoons Dijon-style mustard

6 Tablespoons (90 ml) canola oil

6 Tablespoons (90 ml) walnut oil

¼ teaspoon sea salt

1 ounce (28 g) shallot, peeled

4 cups (80 g) arugula

⅔ cup (80 g) dried cranberries

⅓ cup (36 g) chopped pecans, toasted

1. Place juice, mustard, oils, and shallot into the Vitamix container and secure lid.

2. Select Variable 1.

3. Switch machine to Start and slowly increase speed to Variable 10.

4. Blend for 20 seconds.

5. Toss ½ cup (120 ml) dressing with arugula, cranberries, and pecans.

6. Store remaining dressing refrigerated in an airtight container for 1 to 2 weeks.

Nutritional Information

Amount Per Serving: *Calories 230, Total Fat 18g, Saturated Fat 1.5g, Cholesterol 0mg, Sodium 80mg, Total Carbohydrate 21g, Dietary Fiber 2g, Sugars 15g, Protein 1g*

Vegan   **Vegetarian**   **Dairy-free**   **Gluten-free**

Sautéed Brussels Sprouts

Preparation: 10 minutes | **Processing:** Pulsing
Cook Time: 15 minutes | **Yield:** 4 servings

1 pound (454 g) Brussels sprouts, trimmed

3 Tablespoons (42 g) butter, divided use

3 ounces (85 g) shallots, thinly sliced

2 Tablespoons (30 ml) apple cider vinegar

1 Tablespoon granulated sugar

½ cup (120 ml) water

Salt, to taste

Ground black pepper, to taste

1. Place Brussels sprouts into the Vitamix container, fill with water to the 6 cup (1.4 l) mark and secure lid.

2. Select Variable 8.

3. Pulse 6 times until sprouts are shredded. Drain and set aside.

4. Melt 2 Tablespoons (28 g) butter over medium heat in a large skillet. Add shallots and sauté 3 minutes. Add cider vinegar and sugar; cook 2 minutes, stirring frequently. Remove to a plate.

5. Add remaining Tablespoon of butter and increase heat to medium-high. Add Brussels sprouts and season to taste with salt and pepper. Cook 5 minutes. Add water and cook 5 additional minutes. Stir in cooked shallots.

Nutritional Information

Amount Per Serving: Calories 150, Total Fat 9g, Saturated Fat 6g, Cholesterol 25mg, Sodium 105mg, Total Carbohydrate 18g, Dietary Fiber 4g, Sugars 6g, Protein 5g

Vegetarian **Gluten-free**

Whole-Grain Saffron Polenta

Preparation: 20 minutes | ***Processing:*** 1 minute plus Pulsing | ***Cook Time:*** 35 minutes | ***Yield:*** 4 servings

2 cups (416 g) popcorn kernels, or 1 cup (122 g) polenta (coarse cornmeal)

2 Tablespoons (30 ml) olive oil

1 cup (160 g) chopped onion

4 cups (960 ml) Homemade Chicken or Vegetable Stock (page 162–163)

¾ teaspoon kosher salt

½ teaspoon saffron threads

1 ½ cups (246 g) frozen corn kernels, thawed

Salt and ground black pepper, to taste

1. If starting with whole popcorn kernels, place 2 cups (480 g) into the Vitamix container and secure lid.

2. Select Variable 1.

3. Switch machine to Start and slowly increase speed to Variable 10.

4. Blend for 1 minute. Measure out 1 cup (122 g). Place left over cornmeal into a sealed container and store in a cool, dry place.

5. Heat oil in a large saucepan over medium-low heat. Add onion; cover and cook 5 to 8 minutes.

6. Add broth, salt, and saffron. Bring to a boil then add in polenta. Cook, whisking constantly until it boils and starts to thicken, 2 to 3 minutes. Reduce heat to low. Simmer 10 minutes, stirring occasionally. Cover; simmer until cooked through and very thick, about 10 minutes longer.

7. Place thawed corn kernels into the Vitamix container and secure lid.

8. Select Variable 2.

9. Pulse 4 times. Remove lid. Scrape down the sides of the container with a spatula and secure lid. Pulse 2 more times.

10. Stir into cooked polenta. Season to taste with salt and pepper if necessary.

Nutritional Information

Amount Per Serving: *Calories 290, Total Fat 7g, Saturated Fat 1g, Cholesterol 5mg, Sodium 370mg, Total Carbohydrate 50g, Dietary Fiber 6g, Sugars 4g, Protein 6g*

Dairy-free   **Gluten-free**

Cornbread

Preparation: 15 minutes | **Processing:** 1 minute 15 seconds | **Bake Time:** 20 minutes | **Yield:** 12 slices

2 cups (416 g) popcorn kernels

1 cup (125 g) all-purpose flour

½ cup (100 g) granulated sugar

1 Tablespoon baking powder

½ teaspoon salt

1 cup (240 ml) milk

¼ cup (56 g) unsalted butter

1 large egg

1. Heat oven to 400°F (200°C). Spray the bottom and sides of an 8-inch (20 cm) square pan with cooking spray or olive oil.

2. Place popcorn kernels into the Vitamix container and secure lid. Select Variable 1.

3. Switch machine to Start and slowly increase speed to Variable 10.

4. Blend for 1 minute.

5. Measure out 1 ¼ cups (153 g) and place into a medium-size mixing bowl. Add flour, sugar, baking powder, and salt to the bowl. Mix lightly by hand and set aside. Place leftover cornmeal into a sealed container and store in a cool, dry place.

6. Place milk, butter, and egg into the Vitamix container in the order listed and secure lid. Select Variable 1.

7. Switch machine to Start and slowly increase speed to Variable 5.

8. Blend for 15 seconds.

9. Pour wet mixture into dry ingredients and stir by hand until flour is moistened. Spread batter into prepared baking pan.

10. Bake 20 minutes or until a toothpick inserted into the center comes out clean.

Nutritional Information

Amount Per Slice: *Calories 170, Total Fat 5g, Saturated Fat 3g, Cholesterol 30mg, Sodium 240mg, Total Carbohydrate 27g, Dietary Fiber 1g, Sugars 9g, Protein 3g*

Vegetarian

Ginger Beet Purée

Preparation: 10 minutes | ***Processing:*** 20–30 seconds | ***Bake Time:*** 2 hours
Yield: 2 ¼ cups (540 ml) (9 servings)

2 ¾ pounds (1.2 kg) fresh beets, about 3 large

2 Tablespoons (30 ml) olive oil

½ cup (72 g) raw almonds

1 ½ Tablespoons chopped fresh ginger root

1 Tablespoon fresh cilantro leaves

1 teaspoon ground ginger

⅛ teaspoon salt

⅛ teaspoon ground black pepper

1. Preheat oven to 425°F (220°C). Clean and cut beets to leave 1 inch (2.5 cm) of stem. Double wrap beets in foil and roast for 2 hours.

2. Trim ends, peel beets, and cut into quarters.

3. Place oil, beets, almonds, fresh ginger, cilantro, ground ginger, salt, and pepper into the Vitamix container in the order listed and secure lid.

4. Select Variable 1.

5. Switch machine to Start and slowly increase speed to Variable 10.

6. Blend for 20 to 30 seconds, using the tamper to press the ingredients into the blades.

Nutritional Information

Amount Per Serving: *Calories 130, Total Fat 7g, Saturated Fat 1g, Cholesterol 0mg, Sodium 140mg, Total Carbohydrate 15g, Dietary Fiber 5g, Sugars 10g, Protein 4g*

Vegan   **Vegetarian**   **Dairy-free**   **Gluten-free**

Roasted Celery Root and Pear Purée

Preparation: 15 minutes | **Processing:** 5 – 10 seconds
Bake Time: 35 – 40 minutes | **Yield:** 6 servings

¾ pound (340 g) celery root, peeled and cut into 1-inch (2.5 cm) chunks

1 garlic clove, peeled

1 ½ cups (240 g) yellow pear, cut into 1-inch (2.5 cm) chunks

5 Tablespoons (75 ml) walnut oil, divided use

½ teaspoon salt

⅔ cup (160 ml) pear juice

¼ cup (60 ml) half & half

freshly grated nutmeg, for garnish

toasted walnuts, for garnish

Chef's Note

To toast walnuts, place in a dry skillet over medium-high heat until deeply browned. Toss pan frequently to prevent burning. Let cool 10 minutes. Place into the Vitamix container and secure lid. Select Variable 5. Pulse 5 times or until chopped.

1. Preheat oven to 400°F (200°C). In a 13-inch x 9-inch (33 cm x 23 cm) baking pan, stir together celery root, garlic clove, pear, 3 Tablespoons (45 ml) walnut oil, and salt.

2. Bake for 35 to 40 minutes, stirring occasionally, until celery root is tender. Remove from oven.

3. Meanwhile, place pear juice, half & half, 2 Tablespoons (30 ml) walnut oil, and garlic clove into the Vitamix container in the order listed. Carefully add roasted vegetables and secure lid.

4. Select Variable 1.

5. Switch machine to Start and slowly increase speed to Variable 10.

6. Blend for 5 to 10 seconds or until slightly smooth, using the tamper to press the ingredients into the blades.

7. Pour purée into bowl. Garnish with sprinkles of fresh nutmeg and a handful of toasted walnuts.

Nutritional Information

Amount Per Serving: *Calories 180, Total Fat 13g, Saturated Fat 2g, Cholesterol 5mg, Sodium 260mg, Total Carbohydrate 16g, Dietary Fiber 2g, Sugars 8g, Protein 1g*

Vegetarian   **Gluten-free**

Curry and Chili Paste with Roasted Vegetables

Preparation: 20 minutes | **Processing:** 5 minutes
Bake Time: 25–30 minutes | **Yield:** 6 servings

1 pound (454 g) fingerling potatoes, washed, cut into 2-inch (5 cm) pieces

2 cups (200 g) cauliflower pieces, trimmed

2 cups (220 g) fresh green beans, trimmed

1 ½ cups (240 g) rough chopped yellow onion

¼ cup (60 ml) vegetable oil

¾ teaspoon salt, divided use

¼ teaspoon plus ⅛ teaspoon ground black pepper, divided use

⅔ cup (160 ml) light coconut milk

1 teaspoon roasted chile paste

¼ teaspoon curry powder

1. Preheat oven to 400°F (200°C). In a 13-inch x 9-inch (33 cm x 23 cm) baking pan, stir together potatoes, cauliflower, green beans, onion, vegetable oil, ½ teaspoon salt, and ¼ teaspoon black pepper.

2. Bake for 25 to 30 minutes, stirring occasionally, until potatoes are tender. Remove from oven; keep warm.

3. Meanwhile, place coconut milk, chile paste, curry powder, ¼ teaspoon salt, and ⅛ teaspoon black pepper into the Vitamix container in the order listed and secure lid.

4. Select Variable 1.

5. Switch machine to Start and slowly increase speed to Variable 10.

6. Blend for 5 minutes or until heavy steam escapes from the vented lid.

7. Pour sauce over vegetables; mix well.

Nutritional Information

Amount Per Serving: *Calories 190, Total Fat 11g, Saturated Fat 2.5g, Cholesterol 0mg, Sodium 550mg, Total Carbohydrate 22g, Dietary Fiber 4g, Sugars 4 g, Protein 3g*

 Vegan   **Vegetarian**   **Dairy-free**   **Gluten-free**

Ingredient IQ

Coconut Craving

Carrying one ingredient throughout a menu is a good way to make sure your flavors complement one another. Just be sure your guests don't have any allergies that will leave them unable to partake in the meal.

Coconut milk is used in each recipe of this spicy menu that mixes a variety of textures and colors. Decorate the table with bright tropical colors and serve Coconut Milk, Curry and Chili Paste with Vegetables alongside Coconut Curry Chicken (See Main Dishes).

To make your own coconut milk, you'll need 2 cups of water and 1 cup of shredded coconut, sweetened or unsweetened.

Place the water and shredded coconut into the Vitamix container, select Variable 1, switch machine to start and slowly increase speed to Variable 10. Blend for 3 minutes and chill or serve immediately.

For a smoother milk, strain through a fine mesh sieve or filtration bag.

Sweet Potato Purée with Maple Bacon and Sage

Preparation: 20 minutes | *Processing:* 20–30 seconds | *Bake Time:* 25–30 minutes | *Yield:* 5 servings

4 cups (530 g) sweet potatoes or yams, peeled and cut into 1-inch (2.5 cm) chunks

1 medium onion, 5 ounces (150 g), peeled and cut into 8 wedges

3 Tablespoons (45 ml) extra virgin olive oil

¾ cup (180 ml) Homemade Chicken Stock (page 163)

2 Tablespoons (8 g) fresh chervil

2 Tablespoons (30 ml) real maple syrup

¾ teaspoon pumpkin pie spice

¼ teaspoon dried marjoram leaves

3 ounces (85 g) maple-flavored bacon, cooked and crumbled for garnish

1 Tablespoon chopped fresh sage, for garnish

1 Tablespoon real maple syrup, for garnish

1. Preheat oven to 400°F (200°C). In a 13-inch x 9-inch (33 cm x 23 cm) baking pan, stir together sweet potatoes, onion, and olive oil. Bake for 25 to 30 minutes, stirring occasionally, until sweet potatoes are tender. Remove from oven.

2. In a small saucepan, heat chicken stock over medium heat until simmering.

3. Carefully place chicken stock, chervil, maple syrup, pumpkin pie spice, and marjoram leaves into the Vitamix container in the order listed. Carefully add roasted sweet potato mixture and secure lid. Select Variable 1.

4. Switch machine to Start and slowly increase speed to Variable 10.

5. Blend for 20 to 30 seconds or until smooth, using the tamper to press the ingredients into the blades.

6. Place in serving bowl. Garnish with bacon, fresh sage, and a drizzle of maple syrup.

Nutritional Information

Amount Per Serving: Calories 300, Total Fat 16g, Saturated Fat 4g, Cholesterol 15mg, Sodium 360mg, Total Carbohydrate 33g, Dietary Fiber 4g, Sugars 15g, Protein 6g

Dairy-free **Gluten-free**

Sweet Potato Pancakes

Preparation: 20 minutes | **Processing:** Pulsing | **Cook Time:** 15 minutes
Yield: 20 mini pancakes (5 servings)

⅓ cup (40 g) whole wheat flour

¼ cup (26 g) flaxseed meal

1 teaspoon baking powder

½ teaspoon salt

½ teaspoon curry powder

¼ cup (60 ml) 2% milk

2 Tablespoons (30 ml)
melted butter

1 large egg

2 Tablespoons (20 g)
chopped onion

2 Tablespoons (2 g)
cilantro leaves

2 cups (266 g) peeled and rough
chopped sweet potato

2 teaspoons vegetable oil

1. In a large bowl, combine flour, flaxseed meal, baking powder, salt, and
   curry powder. Stir by hand to combine. Set aside.

2. Place milk, melted butter, egg, onion, cilantro, and sweet potato into the Vitamix
   container in the order listed and secure lid.

3. Select Variable 10.

4. Pulse 8 times or until sweet potato looks grated. Pour wet mixture into dry
   ingredients and stir by hand to combine.

5. Heat oil in a nonstick skillet over medium heat. Drop batter by rounded Tablespoons.
   Flatten slightly with back of the spoon. Cook 1 ½ minutes or until browned. Flip over and
   gently press down with spatula. Cook an additional 1 ½ minutes or until cooked through.

Nutritional Information

Amount Per Serving (4 Mini Pancakes): *Calories 180, Total Fat 10g, Saturated Fat 3.5g,
Cholesterol 50mg, Sodium 420mg, Total Carbohydrate 19g, Dietary Fiber 4g, Sugars 3g, Protein 5g*

Vegetarian

Polenta Flax Cakes with Rustic Tomato Sauce

Preparation: 20 minutes | **Processing:** 1 minute plus Pulsing | **Cook Time:** 1 hour
Yield: 18 slices and 3 cups (720 ml) sauce (9 servings)

2 cups (416 g) popcorn kernels,
or 1 cup (122 g) whole-grain cornmeal

4 cups (960 ml) water, divided use

1 teaspoon salt

⅓ cup (34 g) flaxseed meal

¼ cup (15 g) fresh parsley leaves

¼ cup (25 g) grated
Parmesan cheese

1 teaspoon whole flaxseed

2 Tablespoons (30 ml) olive oil

2 pounds (908 g) ripe tomatoes,
quartered (approximately
6 tomatoes)

1. If starting with whole popcorn kernels, place 2 cups into the Vitamix container and secure lid. Select Variable 1. Switch machine to Start and slowly increase speed to Variable 10.

2. Blend for 1 minute. Transfer 1 cup (122 g) cornmeal to a medium-size mixing bowl and combine with 1 cup (240 ml) water. Place leftover cornmeal into a sealed container and store in a cool, dry place.

3. Bring 3 cups (720 ml) water to a boil. Add cornmeal mixture and salt, stirring constantly until thickened, 2 minutes. Cover, reduce heat to low, and cook 10 minutes longer, stirring occasionally.

4. Remove from heat, stir in flaxseed meal, parsley, and Parmesan cheese. Spoon into a 9-inch x 5-inch (23 cm x 13 cm) loaf pan. Sprinkle with whole flaxseed and chill for 2 hours.

5. Place 6 tomato quarters into the Vitamix container and secure lid. Select Variable 5. Pulse 6 times. Transfer to a bowl and repeat with remaining tomato quarters.

6. Heat olive oil in a medium pan and add chopped tomatoes. Cook until tomatoes are soft and sauce has thickened, about 12 to 15 minutes. Reduce heat and keep warm.

7. When polenta is chilled, invert loaf pan over a cutting board to remove polenta. Cut into ½-inch-thick (1.3 cm) slices as you would a bread loaf. Heat a lightly oiled, nonstick pan over medium heat. Cook 4 polenta slices at a time, about 5 minutes on each side until golden brown. Keep warm until all slices are cooked. Serve with warm tomato sauce.

Nutritional Information

Amount Per Serving (2 Slices Polenta with ⅓ Cup (80 g) Sauce): *Calories 120, Total Fat 6g, Saturated Fat 1g, Cholesterol 0mg, Sodium 310mg, Total Carbohydrate 16g, Dietary Fiber 4g, Sugars 3g, Protein 4g*

Vegetarian Gluten-free

Mexican Rice

Preparation: 10 minutes | ***Processing:*** 20–30 seconds | ***Cook Time:*** 36–46 minutes
Yield: 8 servings

1 ¾ cups (420 ml) Homemade Vegetable Stock (page 162)

10 ½ ounces (300 g) ripe tomatoes, quartered

2 garlic cloves, peeled, divided use

1 ounce (28 g) wedge yellow onion, peeled

2 Tablespoons (30 ml) canola oil

⅛ teaspoon salt

ground black pepper

1 cup (185 g) uncooked white rice

chopped tomatoes, green chilies, or sliced pimentos, for garnish

1. Place broth, tomatoes, one garlic clove, and onion into the Vitamix container in the order listed and secure lid.

2. Select Variable 1.

3. Switch machine to Start and slowly increase speed to Variable 7.

4. Blend for 20 to 30 seconds. Set aside.

5. Heat oil in a 4-quart saucepan over medium heat. Chop remaining garlic clove and add to the oil. Add rice and cook until rice is golden brown, stirring frequently, about 6 minutes.

6. Stir in tomato mixture, season with ⅛ teaspoon salt and black pepper, and reduce heat to low. Cook, covered until rice is tender and has absorbed all the liquid, 30 to 40 minutes. Remove from heat and let sit covered for 10 minutes.

7. Garnish with chopped tomatoes, green chilies, or sliced pimentos.

Nutritional Information

Amount Per ½ Cup (120g) Serving: *Calories 120, Total Fat 3.5g, Saturated Fat 0g, Cholesterol 0mg, Sodium 40mg, Total Carbohydrate 20g, Dietary Fiber 1g, Sugars 2g, Protein 2g*

Vegan   **Vegetarian**   **Dairy-free**   **Gluten-free**

Sauces

Vegan

Vegetarian

Dairy-free

Gluten-free

Wake up pastas and proteins with fresh, preservative-free sauces. Explore delicious recipes for savory pestos, boldly flavored dipping sauces, and more.

Sauces

PESTOS / SAUCES

Fresh Tomato Sauce

Preparation: 15 minutes | ***Processing:*** 20 seconds | ***Cook Time:*** 35–40 minutes
Yield: 3 ½ cups (840 ml) (7 servings)

6 medium Roma tomatoes, (400 g), quartered

¼ cup (40 g) chopped onion

½ cup (65 g) chopped carrot

2 Tablespoons (30 g) tomato paste

1 garlic clove, peeled

½ teaspoon dried basil

½ teaspoon dried oregano

½ teaspoon fresh lemon juice

½ teaspoon honey

Salt, to taste

Ground black pepper, to taste

1. Place all ingredients into the Vitamix container in the order listed and secure lid.

2. Select Variable 1.

3. Switch machine to Start and slowly increase speed to Variable 10.

4. Blend for 20 seconds.

5. Pour into saucepan and simmer 35 to 40 minutes. Season to taste with salt and pepper, if desired.

Nutritional Information

Amount Per Serving: *Calories 30, Total Fat 0g, Saturated Fat 0g, Cholesterol 0mg, Sodium 25mg, Total Carbohydrate 7g, Dietary Fiber 2g, Sugars 4g, Protein 1g*

Vegetarian   **Dairy-free**   **Gluten-free**

Kale and Basil Pesto

Preparation: 15 minutes | **Processing:** 20–30 seconds
Yield: 1 ¾ cups (420 ml) (14 servings)

1 cup (240 ml) olive oil

1 cup (100 g) grated
Parmesan cheese

3 medium garlic cloves, peeled

2 cups (80 g) fresh basil leaves

2 cups (135 g) fresh kale leaves

3 Tablespoons (25 g) pine nuts

¼ teaspoon kosher salt

Pinch of ground black pepper

1. Place all ingredients into the Vitamix container in the order listed and secure lid.

2. Select Variable 1.

3. Switch machine to Start and slowly increase speed to Variable 5.

4. Blend for 20 to 30 seconds or until desired consistency is reached.

Nutritional Information

Amount Per 2 Tablespoon (30 g) Serving: Calories 190, Total Fat 19g, Saturated Fat 3.5g, Cholesterol 5mg, Sodium 125mg, Total Carbohydrate 2g, Dietary Fiber 0g, Sugars 0g, Protein 3g

Vegetarian **Gluten-free**

Parsley Pesto

Preparation: 15 minutes | ***Processing:*** 20 – 30 seconds | ***Yield:*** 1 ½ cups (360 ml) (12 servings)

1 cup (240 ml) extra virgin olive oil

1 Tablespoon white wine vinegar

1 cup (61 g) packed parsley leaves

⅔ cup (92 g) capers, drained

1 Tablespoon packed fresh
oregano leaves

½ teaspoon crushed red
pepper flakes

2 garlic cloves, peeled

Ground black pepper, to taste

1. Place all ingredients into the Vitamix container in the
   order listed and secure lid.

2. Select Variable 1.

3. Switch machine to Start and slowly increase speed to Variable 5.

4. Blend for 20 to 30 seconds.

5. Serve with grilled vegetables, chicken, or toss with hot cooked pasta.

Nutritional Information

Amount Per 2 Tablespoon (30 g) Serving: *Calories 170, Total Fat 19g, Saturated Fat 2.5g,
Cholesterol 0mg, Sodium 230mg, Total Carbohydrate 1g, Dietary Fiber 0g, Sugars 0g, Protein 0g*

Vegan   **Vegetarian**   **Dairy-free**   **Gluten-free**

Dijon Mint Glaze

Preparation: 10 minutes | *Processing:* 25 – 35 seconds | *Yield:* 1 cup (240 ml) (8 servings)

½ cup (120 g) Dijon-style mustard

½ cup (120 ml) honey

2 Tablespoons (30 g) prepared horseradish

⅓ cup (30 g) fresh mint leaves

1. Place all ingredients into the Vitamix container in the order listed and secure lid.

2. Select Variable 1.

3. Switch machine to Start and slowly increase speed to Variable 6.

4. Blend for 20 to 30 seconds. Stop machine and remove lid. Scrape down the sides of the container with a spatula. Blend an additional 5 seconds.

Nutritional Information

Amount Per 2 Tablespoon (30 ml) Serving: Calories 90, Total Fat 0g, Saturated Fat 0g, Cholesterol 0mg, Sodium 380mg, Total Carbohydrate 21g, Dietary Fiber 1g, Sugars 16g, Protein 0g

Vegetarian **Dairy-free** **Gluten-free**

Red Pepper Dijon Steak Sauce

Preparation: 55 minutes (includes roasting peppers)
Processing: 20–30 seconds
Yield: 3 ¼ cups (780 ml) (26 servings)

3 red bell peppers, 22 ounces (625 g), roasted, peeled, and seeded

¾ cup (180 ml) sherry vinegar

4 ½ Tablespoons (68 ml) Dijon-style mustard

3 Tablespoons (45 ml) prepared horseradish

3 Tablespoons (45 ml) honey

1 ½ Tablespoons molasses

3 teaspoons Worcestershire sauce

1 ½ teaspoons kosher salt

¾ teaspoon ground black pepper

1. Place all ingredients into the Vitamix container in the order listed and secure lid.

2. Select Variable 1.

3. Switch machine to Start and slowly increase speed to Variable 7.

4. Blend for 20 to 30 seconds or until smooth.

Nutritional Information

Amount Per 2 Tablespoon (30 ml) Serving: *Calories 20, Total Fat 0g, Saturated Fat 0g, Cholesterol 0mg, Sodium 190mg, Total Carbohydrate 5g, Dietary Fiber 1g, Sugars 4g, Protein 0g*

Vegetarian   **Dairy-free**   **Gluten-free**

Ingredient IQ

Roasting Peppers

With a sweet, robust flavor, roasted peppers can liven up many dishes and are a staple in many foods like pasta, salad, and sandwiches.

To roast peppers, heat oven to broil. Wash and dry peppers, slice them in half, and remove seeds. Place them on foil or a cookie sheet, skin side up. Allow peppers to broil until skin bubbles and wrinkles (about 5 to 20 minutes, depending on size of the pepper).

Chunky Apple Cranberry Sauce

Preparation: 20 minutes | **Processing:** Pulsing
Cook Time: 20 minutes | **Yield:** 2 cups (480 ml) (8 servings)

3 Tablespoons (45 g) unsalted butter

2 cups (230 g) sliced red onion

¾ cup (180 ml) apple juice

½ cup (120 ml) orange juice

2–3 teaspoons adobo sauce from canned chipotle chilies (optional)

7 ½ ounces (213 g) apple, cut into large chunks

½ cup (55 g) fresh or frozen unsweetened cranberries

Chef's Note

If using the adobo sauce, the flavor goes well with pork. Without adobo, it makes a delicious condiment with poultry.

1. Melt butter in a large skillet. Add onion and sauté over medium heat until lightly browned, 7 minutes.

2. Add juices, apples, cranberries, and adobo sauce to the skillet. Bring to a boil; simmer for 10 minutes.

3. Place mixture into the Vitamix container and secure lid.

4. Select Variable 6.

5. Pulse 6 times until combined.

Nutritional Information

Amount Per Serving: *Calories 80, Total Fat 4.5g, Saturated Fat 3g, Cholesterol 10mg, Sodium 40mg, Total Carbohydrate 12g, Dietary Fiber 1g, Sugars 8g, Protein 1g*

Vegetarian   **Gluten-free**

Spicy Mango Sauce

Preparation: 15 minutes | **Processing:** 15 seconds | **Cook Time:** 12 – 16 minutes
Yield: 1 ¾ cups (420 ml) (14 servings)

2 Tablespoons (30 ml) canola oil

2 ½ ounces (71 g) onion, rough chopped

5 ½ ounces (156 g) red bell pepper,
seeded, rough chopped

3 ½ ounces (100 g) tomato, rough chopped

¾ cup (180 g) hot mango chutney

1. Heat oil in a medium-size saucepan over medium heat. Add onion and bell pepper, cover, and cook 5 to 7 minutes. Add tomato, cover, and cook 5 to 7 minutes. Add chutney, stirring to heat through. Cook for 1 to 2 minutes.

2. Place mixture into the Vitamix container and secure lid.

3. Select Variable 1.

4. Switch machine to Start and slowly increase speed to Variable 5.

5. Blend for 15 seconds.

6. Serve warm with grilled tofu or fish.

Nutritional Information

Amount Per 2 Tablespoon (30 ml) Serving: *Calories 60, Total Fat 3.5g, Saturated Fat 0g, Cholesterol 0mg, Sodium 140mg, Total Carbohydrate 8g, Dietary Fiber 1g, Sugars 1g, Protein 0g*

Vegan   **Vegetarian**   **Dairy-free**   **Gluten-free**

Tomatillo and Pineapple Sauce

Preparation: 25 minutes | **Processing:** 30 seconds plus Pulsing | **Cook Time:** 1 hour 20 minutes
Yield: 4 cups (960 ml) (8 servings)

1 pound (454 g) tomatillos, husked and rinsed

3 ounces (85 g) jalapeños, seeded

4 Tablespoons (56 g) unsalted butter

1 pound (454 g) fresh pineapple, cut into large chunks, core included

1 teaspoon cumin seeds

½ teaspoon ground cinnamon

7 ½ ounces (213 g) Granny Smith apple, cored and halved

2 garlic cloves, peeled

2 Tablespoons (30 ml) olive oil

¼ cup (60 ml) mango nectar

1 Tablespoon apple cider vinegar

1 Tablespoon granulated sugar

1. Bring a 4-quart saucepan of water to a boil and add tomatillos and jalapeños. Cook until tender, about 10 minutes. Drain.

2. Heat butter in a 12-inch (30 cm) skillet over high heat. Add pineapple, cumin, cinnamon, and apple. Cook, stirring constantly until beginning to caramelize, about 5 minutes. Reduce heat to medium-low and cook, stirring frequently until fruit is tender, about 20 minutes. Remove from heat and add ½ cup (120 ml) water, scraping the bottom of the skillet to incorporate brown bits.

3. Add sauce to the Vitamix container and secure lid. Select Variable 1.

4. Switch machine to Start and slowly increase speed to Variable 7. Blend for 30 seconds. Stop machine and remove lid.

5. Add tomatillos and jalapeños to the Vitamix container and secure lid. Pulse 7 to 8 times until slightly chunky. Set aside.

6. Heat oil in a 6-quart saucepan over high heat; add salsa and ½ cup (120 ml) water. Bring to a boil. Reduce heat to low and cook, stirring until thickened, about 45 minutes.

7. Add mango nectar, vinegar, and sugar and cook for 1 minute. Remove from heat and let cool before serving.

Nutritional Information

Amount Per Serving: Calories 160, Total Fat 10g, Saturated Fat 4g, Cholesterol 15mg, Sodium 0mg, Total Carbohydrate 18g, Dietary Fiber 2g, Sugars 13 g, Protein 1g

Vegetarian   **Gluten-free**

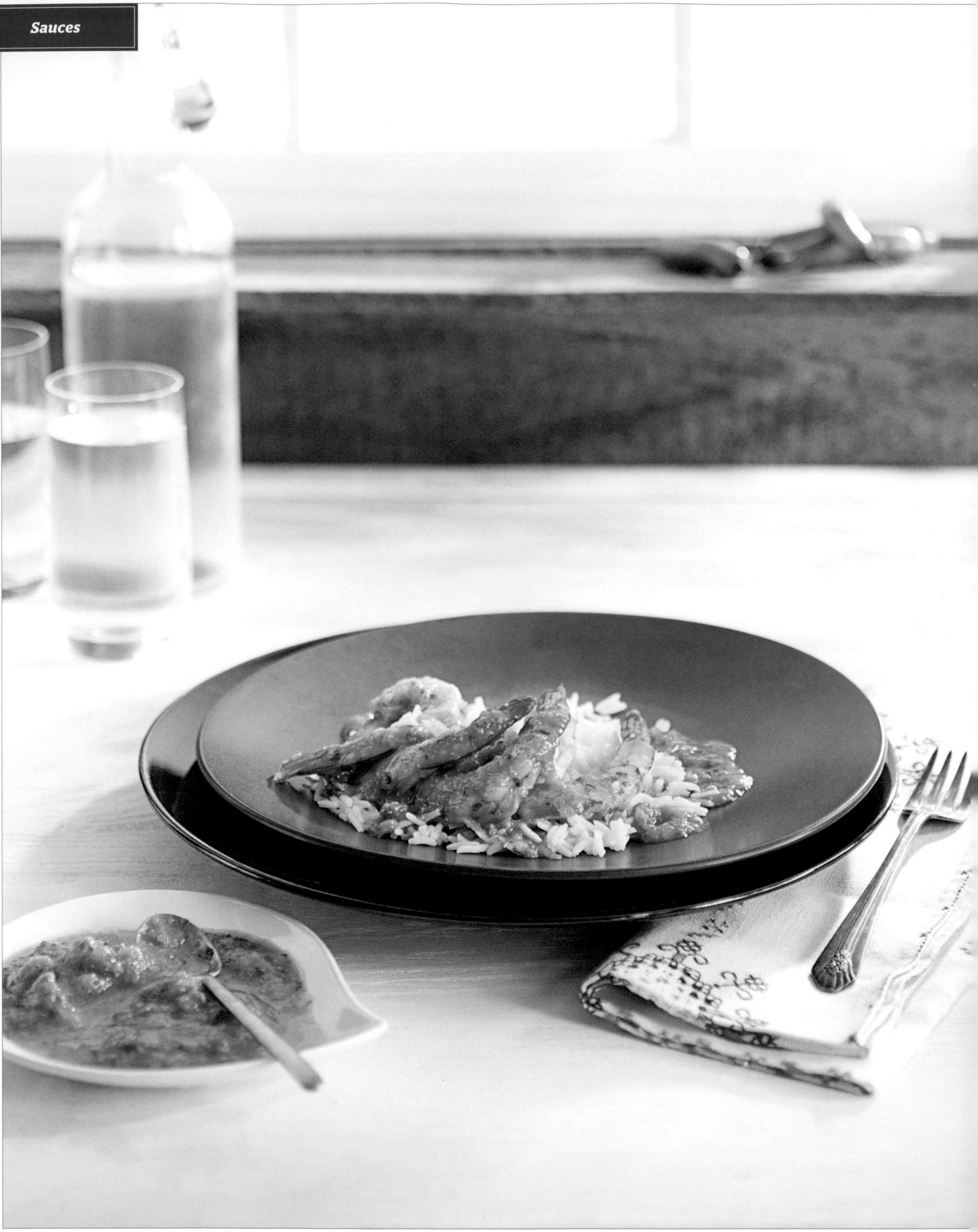

Pineapple Chili Sambal

Preparation: 20 minutes | **Processing:** Pulsing
Yield: 2 ¾ cups (660 ml) (132 servings)

2 cups (330 g) fresh
pineapple chunks

½ cup (8 g) fresh cilantro leaves

3 Tablespoons (45 g) chile paste

3 Tablespoons (45 g) chopped
fresh ginger root

6 Tablespoons (90 g)
white miso paste

6 Tablespoons (90 ml)
rice wine vinegar

¼ cup (55 g) light brown sugar

2 teaspoons toasted sesame oil

Chef's Note

This recipe is extremely spicy. Use ½–1 teaspoon at a time. If the consistency is too thin, add more pineapple chunks to thicken.

1. Place all ingredients into the Vitamix container in the order listed and secure lid.

2. Select Variable 7.

3. Pulse 5 times or until desired consistency is reached.

4. Store refrigerated for up to 1 month.

Nutritional Information

Amount Per 1 teaspoon Serving: *Calories 5, Total Fat 0g, Saturated Fat 0g, Cholesterol 0mg, Sodium 40mg, Total Carbohydrate 1g, Dietary Fiber 0g, Sugars 1g, Protein 0g*

Vegan   **Vegetarian**   **Dairy-free**

Chef's Note

Drizzle this *Green Curry Sauce over seared striped bass, or serve it as a dip for Crab Cakes with Sweet Chili Dipping Sauce (See Appetizers).*

Green Curry Sauce

Preparation: 10 minutes | **Processing:** 15 seconds
Yield: 1 ½ cups (360 ml) (6 servings)

2 teaspoons sesame oil

¼ cup (24 g) peeled, chopped fresh ginger root

2 garlic cloves, peeled and sliced

¼ cup (60 ml) dry white wine

1 Tablespoon fresh lime juice

2 teaspoons green curry paste

13 ½-ounce (403 ml) can light coconut milk

½ teaspoon fish sauce (preferably Nam Pla)

½ cup (8 g) cilantro leaves

Kosher salt, to taste

Freshly ground black pepper, to taste

Lime, to taste

1. In a small saucepan, heat sesame oil over medium heat. Add the ginger and garlic and sauté for 30 seconds. Add white wine and lime juice and reduce to almost dry. Add curry paste, coconut milk, and fish sauce and reduce to 1 cup (240 ml) liquid. Let cool 10 minutes.

2. Place cooked mixture and cilantro into the Vitamix container and secure lid.

3. Select Variable 1.

4. Switch machine to Start and slowly increase speed to Variable 10.

5. Blend for 15 seconds.

Nutritional Information

Amount Per Serving: *Calories 70, Total Fat 6g, Saturated Fat 4g, Cholesterol 0mg, Sodium 95mg, Total Carbohydrate 3g, Dietary Fiber 0g, Sugars 0g, Protein 0g*

Dairy-free

Trapanese Pesto Sauce

Preparation: 15 minutes | **Processing:** Pulsing plus 40 seconds
Cook Time: 5–7 minutes | **Yield:** 3 cups (720 ml) (24 servings)

¾ cup (69 g) sliced almonds, toasted

1 pint (454 g) cherry tomatoes

½ cup (12 g) lightly packed basil leaves

½ cup (50 g) finely grated Parmesan cheese

2 Tablespoons (18 g) golden raisins

2 Tablespoons (17 g) capers, drained

¼ teaspoon crushed red pepper flakes

3 anchovy filets in oil, drained

2 garlic cloves, peeled

1 large jalapeño, 1 ½ ounces (43 g), seeded

½ teaspoon kosher salt

⅛ teaspoon ground black pepper

6 Tablespoons (90 ml) extra virgin olive oil

1. Toast almonds over medium heat in a dry skillet. Toss or stir frequently to prevent burning. Toast until the almonds are a light golden-brown, 5 to 7 minutes. Set aside.

2. Place tomatoes into the Vitamix container and secure lid. Select Variable 3.

3. Pulse 4 to 5 times. Remove lid and add almonds, basil, Parmesan, raisins, capers, red pepper flakes, anchovy filets, garlic, jalapeño, salt, and pepper and secure lid. Select Variable 1.

4. Switch machine to Start and remove lid plug. Slowly pour oil through the lid plug opening. Blend for 30 seconds. Stop machine and remove lid. Scrape down the sides of the container with a spatula and secure lid. Blend an additional 10 seconds.

5. Toss with hot cooked pasta, such as fusilli or bow ties, or use as a dip.

Nutritional Information

Amount Per 2 Tablespoon (30 g) Serving: *Calories 60, Total Fat 5g, Saturated Fat 1g, Cholesterol 0mg, Sodium 80mg, Total Carbohydrate 2g, Dietary Fiber 1g, Sugars 1g, Protein 2g*

Gluten-free

Pesto 101

Around the world, different cultures infuse their sauces with the seasonings of their surroundings. From pungent spices to fresh herbs to juicy fruits, the ingredients in a sauce can bring wonderful flavors to any meal.

Traditional pesto sauce originates from Genoa, Italy and contains basil, pine nuts, garlic, olive oil, and Parmesan cheese, though there are several variations that swap these ingredients for others.

One example is Trapanese pesto (pesto alla trapanese), named after Trapani, the Italian city in which it became popular. There are many ways to flavor this pesto, but the main difference is the use of almonds in place of pine nuts.

Chef's Note

Toss 1 pound cooked noodles and blanched vegetables with 1 ½ cups sesame paste.

Sesame Paste

Preparation: 10 minutes | **Processing:** 30 seconds
Yield: 1 ½ cups (360 ml) (6 servings)

½ cup (120 ml) rice bran oil or peanut oil

1 Tablespoon black sesame oil

3 Tablespoons (45 ml) rice wine vinegar

3 Tablespoons (45 ml) soy sauce

1 Tablespoon rice wine or saké

1 cup (130 g) white sesame seeds, toasted

2 Tablespoons (25 g) fine sugar

1. Place all ingredients into the Vitamix container in the order listed and secure lid.

2. Select Variable 1.

3. Switch machine to Start and slowly increase speed to Variable 8.

4. Blend for 30 seconds.

5. Store refrigerated in an airtight jar.

Nutritional Information

Amount Per Serving: Calories 330, Total Fat 31g, Saturated Fat 5g, Cholesterol 0mg, Sodium 580mg, Total Carbohydrate 11g, Dietary Fiber 3g, Sugars 5g, Protein 4g

Vegan **Vegetarian** **Dairy-free**

Main Dishes

Vegan

Vegetarian

Dairy-free

Gluten-free

Find healthy meals for quick weeknight dinners, as well as inspiration for your next party or gathering. Make dinner a family event with Thin Crust Pineapple Pizza, or impress guests with Butternut Squash Ravioli with Hazelnut Pesto.

Main Dishes

BEEF / FISH / PORK / POULTRY / VEGETARIAN

Thin Crust Pineapple Pizza

Preparation: 25 minutes | ***Processing:*** Pulsing
Bake Time: 35 minutes | ***Yield:*** 8 slices (1 large pizza)

Toppings:

1 ½ cups (248 g) diced
fresh pineapple

1 teaspoon brown sugar

12 ounces (340 g) onion, sliced

1 teaspoon fresh rosemary

1 teaspoon fresh thyme

2 Tablespoons (30 ml) olive oil

3 ½ ounces (100 g) Romano
and Asiago cheese chunks

¼ cup (60 g) mayonnaise

1 Tablespoon chopped fresh basil

2 small garlic cloves,
peeled and chopped

¼ cup (28 g) sun-dried
tomatoes, sliced thin

1 ½ teaspoons crushed red
pepper flakes

1 Tablespoon chopped fresh basil

Thin crust pizza dough:

3 lightly filled and leveled cups
(375 g) all-purpose flour

1 ¾ teaspoons instant
fast rise yeast

1 ¼ teaspoons salt

8–11 ounces (240–320 ml)
hot water

3 ¾ teaspoons olive oil

1. Preheat oven to 400°F (200°C). Combine pineapple and brown sugar in a baking pan and roast for 10 minutes. Toss sliced onions with herbs and olive oil. Roast on a separate baking sheet 10 minutes or until slightly browned. Set aside.

2. Place Romano and Asiago cheese chunks into the Vitamix container and secure lid.

3. Select Variable 3.

4. Pulse 20 times. Measure out 1 ¼ cups (125 g) grated cheese. Set aside.

5. Combine mayonnaise, basil, and garlic by hand in a small bowl. Set aside.

6. Preheat oven to 425°F (220°C).

Thin Crust Pineapple Pizza *continues on page 270*

Bright Idea

Make-Your-Own-Pizza Night

Instead of ordering in next Friday night, turn your kitchen into a pizza parlor. Set up prep stations where everyone can roll out pizza dough and assemble their own made-to-order pies.

For planning ahead, prepare two batches of dough. Shape unused dough and place on a cookie sheet in the freezer until firm, remove, wrap well, and freeze up to 1 month. Then, thaw in the fridge the night before use. Dough can be used for another pizza night or rolled into bread sticks and served with pasta.

Experiment with unique flavor combinations and use your favorite fresh herbs such as oregano, rosemary, thyme, and basil. There are also plenty of cheese varieties to complement your toppings.

continued from page 269

Thin Crust Pineapple Pizza

7. Place flour, yeast, and salt into the Vitamix container in the order listed and secure lid.

8. Select Variable 1.

9. Switch machine to Start and slowly increase speed to Variable 8. Blend for 5 seconds. Turn machine off and remove lid plug.

10. Select Variable 3.

11. Pulse about 60 short times in 45 seconds while slowly adding oil and water through the lid plug opening until a ball forms.

12. After ball has formed, Pulse continuously for 10 to 15 seconds.

13. With floured hands, remove dough and form into a round ball. Place in a greased bowl, turning over to grease all sides. Let rise 10 minutes for a thin crust. Stretch into pizza and spread mayonnaise mixture as a sauce. Top with roasted pineapple and onions, and sprinkle with grated cheeses. Bake for 12 to 15 minutes.

Nutritional Information

Amount Per Slice: *Calories 370, Total Fat 16g, Saturated Fat 4g, Cholesterol 15mg, Sodium 600mg, Total Carbohydrate 46g, Dietary Fiber 3g, Sugars 5g, Protein 10g*

Vegetarian

Zucchini Burgers

Preparation: 15 minutes | *Processing:* Pulsing | *Cook Time:* 6 minutes | *Yield:* 17 patties

2 pounds (908 g) zucchini, cut into large chunks

1 large onion, peeled and quartered, about 1 ¼ cups (195 g) chopped

1 ½ cups (180 g) Italian seasoned dry breadcrumbs

3 large eggs

½ cup (50 g) shredded Romano or Parmesan cheese

½ teaspoon garlic powder

½ teaspoon onion powder

½ teaspoon dried parsley

½ teaspoon dried basil

½ teaspoon dried oregano

¼ cup (60 ml) canola oil

1. Place zucchini into the Vitamix container, float with water and secure lid.

2. Select Variable 6.

3. Pulse 5 times until chopped. Strain in a colander. Place towel or paper towel over top to pat dry.

4. Place onion into the Vitamix container and secure lid.

5. Select Variable 4.

6. Pulse 4 to 5 times to evenly chop. Combine zucchini, onion, breadcrumbs, eggs, cheese, and spices in a large-size mixing bowl and stir until evenly combined.

7. Heat a large 12-inch (30 cm) heavy-bottomed skillet over medium-high heat. Pour ¼ cup (60 ml) oil in pan. When oil is hot, measure ¼ cup (60 g) portions of the zucchini mixture into the pan.

8. Spread gently to form a patty. Cook 3 minutes or until the underside is crispy and dark brown.

9. Flip and cook an additional 3 minutes. Remove to a paper towel-lined plate.

Nutritional Information

Amount Per Patty: Calories 110, Total Fat 6g, Saturated Fat 1.5g, Cholesterol 35mg, Sodium 240mg, Total Carbohydrate 10g, Dietary Fiber 1g, Sugars 2g, Protein 5g

Vegetarian

Jerk Chicken with Pineapple Mango Salsa

Preparation: 20 minutes | **Processing:** 40 seconds plus Pulsing | **Cook Time:** 10 minutes
Yield: 1 ½ cups (360 ml) jerk seasoning; 2 ½ cups (600 ml) salsa (8 servings)

Jerk Chicken:

2 cups (375 g) frozen unsweetened pineapple chunks, thawed, or 2 cups (330 g) fresh pineapple chunks

1 medium onion, 3 ounces (85 g), rough chopped

2 teaspoons dried thyme

2 teaspoons garlic powder

½ teaspoon ground allspice

½ teaspoon ground cinnamon

½ teaspoon ground black pepper

¼ teaspoon cayenne pepper

8 (3-ounce/85 g) boneless skinless chicken breasts

Pineapple Mango Salsa:

2 cups (330 g) fresh pineapple chunks

2 cups (330 g) fresh mango chunks

¼ cup (5 g) packed fresh cilantro leaves

1 ½ teaspoons lime zest

⅛ large jalapeño

1. Place pineapple, onion, thyme, garlic powder, allspice, cinnamon, black pepper, and cayenne pepper into the Vitamix container and secure lid.

2. Select Variable 1.

3. Switch machine to Start and slowly increase speed to Variable 5.

4. Blend for 30 seconds. Stop machine and remove lid. Scrape down the sides of the container with a spatula and secure lid. Blend an additional 10 seconds.

5. Rub mixture onto chicken breasts. Grill chicken, turning halfway through cooking until center reaches an internal temperature of 170°F (77°C).

6. Serve chicken breasts topped with Pineapple Mango Salsa (see next page).

Jerk Chicken with Pineapple Mango Salsa continues on page 274

continued from page 272

Jerk Chicken with Pineapple Mango Salsa

7. Place all salsa ingredients into the Vitamix container and secure lid.

8. Select Variable 6.

9. Pulse 10 times until all ingredients are chopped. If large pieces still remain, reduce speed to Variable 3 and Pulse a few more times.

Nutritional Information

Amount Per Serving (chicken breast with ⅓ cup (80 ml) salsa): *Calories 190, Total Fat 2.5g, Saturated Fat 0.5g, Cholesterol 55mg, Sodium 100mg, Total Carbohydrate 23g, Dietary Fiber 2g, Sugars 19g, Protein 19g*

Dairy-free   Gluten-free

Curried Tropical Stir-Fry

Preparation: 20 minutes | **Processing:** 6 minutes 10 seconds
Cook Time: 40 minutes plus marinade time | **Yield:** 6 servings

2 Tablespoons (30 ml) soy sauce

1 Tablespoon curry powder

2 Tablespoons (30 ml)
vegetable oil

2 Tablespoons (30 ml)
sesame oil

6 (5-ounce/142 g) boneless
skinless chicken breast halves,
sliced ¼-inch (0.6 cm) thick

1 cup (240 ml) pineapple juice

⅔ cup (160 ml) apricot nectar

1 Tablespoon white vinegar

¼ cup (40 g) potato starch mixed
with ⅓ cup (80 ml) apricot nectar

6 ounces (170 g) red bell pepper,
cut into ½-inch (1.3 cm) pieces

2 Tablespoons (30 ml)
vegetable oil

1 cup (165 g) fresh pineapple
chunks, small dice

4 cups (632 g) cooked brown rice

⅓ cup (30 g) sliced
almonds, toasted

⅓ cup (33 g) sliced green onions

1. Place soy sauce, curry, vegetable oil, and sesame oil into the Vitamix container in the order listed and secure lid.

2. Select Variable 1.

3. Switch machine to Start and slowly increase speed to Variable 3.

4. Blend for 10 seconds.

5. Place chicken in a bowl and pour marinade over. Refrigerate for 1 to 4 hours.

6. Place pineapple juice, apricot nectar, and vinegar into the Vitamix container and secure lid.

7. Select Variable 1.

8. Switch machine to Start and slowly increase speed to Variable 10.

9. Blend for 5 minutes.

Curried Tropical Stir-Fry continues on page 276

continued from page 275

Curried Tropical Stir-Fry

10. Reduce speed to Variable 1, remove lid plug, and pour apricot potato starch mixture through the lid plug opening. Replace lid plug and slowly increase speed to Variable 10. Blend for 1 minute. Set aside.

11. Sauté peppers in 2 Tablespoons (30 ml) vegetable oil for 10 minutes until tender. Transfer to a plate. Add chicken to skillet in batches, cooking until chicken is no longer pink and juices run clear.

12. Mix cooked chicken with bell peppers, pineapple, and apricot sauce. Serve over cooked rice, and top with a sprinkle of toasted almonds and green onions.

Nutritional Information

Amount Per Serving: *Calories 560, Total Fat 21g, Saturated Fat 2.5g, Cholesterol 90mg, Sodium 500mg, Total Carbohydrate 59g, Dietary Fiber 4g, Sugars 13g, Protein 35g*

Dairy-free

Brazilian Chicken Salad

Preparation: 20 minutes | ***Processing:*** Pulsing plus 20 seconds
Yield: 5 ¾ cups (1.4 kg) (11 ½ servings)

2 pounds (908 g) skinless boneless chicken breast, cooked, cut into 2-inch (5 cm) pieces, cooled

1 (11-ounce / 312 g) can mandarin oranges, drained

½ of a 15 ¼-ounce (432 g) can tropical mixed fruit, drained

½ cup (54 g) slivered almonds, toasted

1 ½ cups (360 g) low-fat mayonnaise

2 Tablespoons (12 g) lemon zest

2 Tablespoons (30 ml) fresh lemon juice

1 teaspoon garlic powder

1 teaspoon ground ginger

½ teaspoon cayenne pepper

Sea salt, to taste

1. Place chicken into the Vitamix container and secure lid. Select Variable 6.

2. Pulse 3 to 5 times. Transfer to a large-size mixing bowl. Stir in mandarin oranges, tropical mixed fruit, and slivered almonds.

3. Place mayonnaise, lemon zest, lemon juice, garlic powder, ground ginger, and cayenne pepper into the Vitamix container in the order listed and secure lid. Select Variable 2.

4. Switch machine to Start and blend for 10 seconds. Stop machine and remove lid. Scrape down the sides of the container with a spatula and secure lid. Switch machine to Start and blend an additional 10 seconds.

5. Add sauce to the fruit and chicken mixture. Stir by hand until combined. Season to taste with salt.

6. Serve ½ cup (188 g) chicken salad on baby spinach greens or use as a sandwich filling.

Nutritional Information

Amount Per Serving: *Calories 260, Total Fat 15g, Saturated Fat 2g, Cholesterol 60mg, Sodium 290mg, Total Carbohydrate 13g, Dietary Fiber 1g, Sugars 9g, Protein 18g*

Gluten-free

Macaroni with Cheese Sauce

Preparation: 15 minutes | **Processing:** 4–5 minutes
Bake Time: 30 minutes | **Yield:** 6 cups (1.4 kg) (6 servings)

Cheese Sauce:

2 cups (210 g) elbow
macaroni, uncooked

¼ cup (60 g) unsalted butter

¼ cup (30 g) all-purpose flour

¼ teaspoon salt

1 ⅓ cups (320 ml) 2% milk

½ teaspoon yellow mustard

1 ½ cups (173 g) cubed mild
Cheddar cheese or other
mild yellow cheese

Crumb Topping:

2 slices whole wheat bread

1 teaspoon unsalted butter

Dash of garlic powder

Dash of ground black pepper

Dash of dried oregano

Dash of onion powder

Dash of cayenne pepper

1. Preheat oven to 350°F (180°C).

2. Cook macaroni as directed on package. Drain.

3. Spray an 8-inch x 8-inch (20 cm x 20 cm) baking dish with vegetable cooking spray and add macaroni to dish.

4. Place butter, flour, salt, milk, and mustard into the Vitamix container in the order listed and secure lid.

5. Select Variable 1.

6. Switch machine to Start and slowly increase speed to Variable 10.

7. Blend for 4 minutes or until steam escapes from the vented lid. As mixture thickens, it will not splash as much.

8. Reduce speed to Variable 1 and remove lid plug. Add cheese through the lid plug opening.

9. Blend for 30 seconds.

Macaroni with Cheese Sauce continues on page 280

Ingredient IQ

Simple Salting

Just as there is a wide variety of herbs and spices, there are many different types of flavor-enhancing salts. Depending on what you cook and the desired result, salt can transform a meal by adding texture, zest, and balance to a range of foods.

Salt can be thought of as divided into three categories: table salt, regular sea and kosher salts, and finishing salts. Each varies in consistency, flavor, and price, based on how the salt is harvested.

Kosher salt, for instance, is excellent for pinching over foods, sprinkling into pasta water, and adding to marinades. With salt crystals slightly larger than those of ordinary table salt, kosher salt is coarse and adds bursts of salty flavor to the foods it complements. Because it's so granular, it doesn't always dissolve in batters, which is why it's best to use refined sea salts for baking.

Finishing salts, such as Fleur de Sel, are best suited for adding to food just before serving. Although slightly more expensive, a little goes a long way when using these versatile salts.

continued from page 279

Macaroni with Cheese Sauce

10. Pour mixture over macaroni and mix thoroughly.

11. Toast and butter 2 pieces of bread and cut into quarters.

12. Select Variable 2.

13. Switch machine to Start and remove lid plug.

14. Drop bread through the lid plug opening. Blend until desired consistency of bread crumbs is reached. Transfer to a bowl and stir in seasonings.

15. Cover macaroni with crumb topping mixture and bake uncovered until top is golden-brown, about 30 minutes.

Nutritional Information

Amount Per Serving: *Calories 420, Total Fat 21g, Saturated Fat 13g, Cholesterol 60mg, Sodium 370mg, Total Carbohydrate 39g, Dietary Fiber 2g, Sugars 5g, Protein 15g*

Vegetarian

Chipotle BBQ Ribs

Preparation: 20 minutes | ***Processing:*** 20 seconds | ***Cook Time:*** 3 hours – 3 hours 55 minutes
Yield: 6 cups (1.4 kg) (6 servings)

3 ½ pounds (1.6 kg) pork loin back
ribs or meaty pork spareribs

1 cup (245 g) no salt added tomato sauce

1 cup (240 g) barbecue sauce

2 canned chipotle chilies in adobo sauce

2 Tablespoons (16 g) cornstarch

2 Tablespoons (30 ml) water

1. Preheat broiler. Cut ribs into two rib portions. Place ribs on the unheated rack of a broiler pan. Broil 6 inches (15 cm) from the heat, about 10 minutes or until brown, turning once. Transfer ribs to a 4 to 5 quart slow cooker.

2. Place tomato sauce, barbecue sauce, and chipotle chilies into the Vitamix container and secure lid.

3. Select Variable 1.

4. Switch machine to Start and slowly increase speed to Variable 3.

5. Blend for 20 seconds. Pour over ribs in the slow cooker.

6. Cover and cook on High for 3 to 3 ½ hours. Transfer ribs to a serving platter, reserving cooking liquid. Cover ribs to keep warm. Skim fat from cooking liquid.

7. Turn slow cooker to High heat. Combine cornstarch and water in a small bowl. Stir into liquid in the slow cooker. Cover and cook 15 minutes, or until thickened. Serve ribs with sauce.

Nutritional Information

Amount Per Serving (2 Ribs): *Calories 580, Total Fat 37g, Saturated Fat 13g, Cholesterol 160mg, Sodium 500mg, Total Carbohydrate 17g, Dietary Fiber 1g, Sugars 13g, Protein 44g*

Dairy-free

Turkey Burgers with Mixed Veggies

Preparation: 10 minutes | **Processing:** Pulsing plus 5 seconds | **Cook Time:** 15 minutes | **Yield:** 4 burgers

1 medium carrot, 2 ½ ounces (71 g), cut into 3 pieces

2 green onions, cut into 2-inch (5 cm) pieces

3 Tablespoons (21 g) dry bread crumbs

¼ teaspoon Italian seasoning

⅛ teaspoon ground black pepper

12 ounces (340 g) ground turkey breast

4 sprouted whole grain hamburger buns, split and toasted

½ cup (139 g) Guacamole (page 180)

1 cup (30 g) mixed baby greens

1. Place carrot pieces into the Vitamix container and secure lid. Select Variable 5.

2. Pulse 10 times to chop finely. Do not remove. Select Variable 2 and remove lid plug.

3. Switch machine to Start and drop onion pieces through the lid plug opening. Stop machine and remove lid.

4. To the carrot and onion mixture, add bread crumbs, spices, and turkey breast and secure lid. Select Variable 4.

5. Pulse 10 times until mixture is fully combined. Form into 4 large patties.

6. Grill patties uncovered over medium heat, 350°F (180°C), for 12 to 15 minutes or until patties are done, turning once halfway through.

7. Serve on hamburger buns topped with guacamole and baby greens.

Nutritional Information

Amount Per Burger: *Calories 340, Total Fat 6g, Saturated Fat 0.5g, Cholesterol 35mg, Sodium 400mg, Total Carbohydrate 43g, Dietary Fiber 9g, Sugars 2g, Protein 32g*

Dairy-free

Shallot Oyster Pork Satay

Preparation: 15 minutes | **Processing:** 30 seconds
Cook Time: 5 minutes | **Chill Time:** 2–4 hours
Yield: 2 cups (480 ml) sauce (8 servings)

6 Tablespoons (90 ml) canola oil

¼ cup (60 ml) oyster sauce

¼ cup (19 g) chopped lemongrass

¼ cup (32 g) toasted
sesame seeds

2 Tablespoons (30 ml) fish sauce

2 teaspoons granulated sugar

3 ounces (85 g) shallots

2 garlic cloves, peeled

1 pound (454 g) pork strips,
1-inch x ¼-inch (2.5 cm x 0.6 cm)

16 wooden skewers, soaked
in water for 30 minutes

Chef's Note

Soak skewers in water for 30 minutes prior to cooking to prevent them from burning. If unable to grill during the winter months, you can sauté instead. Heat 1 Tablespoon olive oil over medium-high heat. Add pork and sauté for 3 to 4 minutes per side or until cooked through.

1. Place oil, oyster sauce, lemongrass, sesame seeds, fish sauce, sugar, shallots, and garlic into the Vitamix container in the order listed and secure lid.

2. Select Variable 1.

3. Switch machine to Start and slowly increase speed to Variable 5.

4. Blend for 30 seconds.

5. Combine sauce with pork strips and chill for 2 to 4 hours.

6. Fold a pork strip onto itself and insert skewer through the center, stretching the meat down the length of the skewer.

7. Grill until lightly charred, about 5 minutes.

Nutritional Information

Amount Per Serving: *Calories 230, Total Fat 19g, Saturated Fat 3g, Cholesterol 25mg, Sodium 630mg, Total Carbohydrate 5g, Dietary Fiber 1g, Sugars 2g, Protein 8g*

Dairy-free

Ground Turkey Sloppy Joes

Preparation: 30 minutes | ***Processing:*** Pulsing plus 30 seconds
Cook Time: 25 minutes | ***Yield:*** 8 servings

¼ cup (30 g) shelled pistachios

6 Tablespoons (90 ml)
vegetable oil, divided use

1 Tablespoon chopped
fresh ginger root

2 garlic cloves, peeled and halved

½ jalapeño pepper, chopped

1 teaspoon garam masala

½ teaspoon paprika

1 (15-ounce/425 g) can
tomato sauce

2 Tablespoons (30 ml) water

¼ cup (36 g) raisins

1 teaspoon cumin seeds

1 medium onion,
5 ounces (142 g), diced

1 medium red bell pepper,
8 ounces (227 g), seeded
and diced

⅛ teaspoon cayenne pepper

Kosher salt, to taste

1 pound (454 g) ground turkey

½ teaspoon honey

¼ cup (60 ml) half & half

¼ cup (4 g) chopped
cilantro leaves

8 sesame buns

1. Place pistachios into the Vitamix container and secure lid.

2. Select Variable 4.

3. Pulse 3 times to chop. Set aside.

4. Heat vegetable oil in a small saucepan over medium heat. Add ginger, garlic,
   and jalapeño. Cook for 1 minute. Remove from heat.

5. Place cooked mixture, garam masala, paprika, tomato sauce, and 2 Tablespoons (30 ml)
   water into the Vitamix container in the order listed and secure lid.

6. Select Variable 4.

7. Switch machine to Start and slowly increase speed to Variable 10.

Ground Turkey Sloppy Joes *continues on page 286*

continued from page 285

Ground Turkey Sloppy Joes

8. Blend for 30 seconds. Reserve.

9. To prepare the sloppy joes, heat 2 Tablespoons (30 ml) vegetable oil in a large skillet over medium heat. Add the raisins and chopped pistachios. Cook until the raisins swell, about 1 minute. Remove from skillet.

10. Add the remaining 4 Tablespoons oil to the skillet and add cumin seeds, onion, and bell pepper. Cook until softened, about 5 minutes. Add cayenne pepper, salt to taste, and turkey, cooking until opaque, about 5 minutes. Break up turkey as you cook to form small crumbles.

11. Add reserved sauce to the skillet. Stir and bring to a boil, then reduce heat to low and simmer until mixture thickens slightly, about 10 minutes.

12. Stir in honey, half & half, raisins, and pistachios. Stir in chopped cilantro before serving. Serve on toasted sesame seed buns.

Nutritional Information

Amount Per Serving: *Calories 440, Total Fat 22g, Saturated Fat 4.5g, Cholesterol 45mg, Sodium 690mg, Total Carbohydrate 43g, Dietary Fiber 3g, Sugars 11g, Protein 19g*

Chop Chop Pocket Sandwiches

Preparation: 15 minutes | **Processing:** Pulsing | **Yield:** 8 sandwiches

1 cup (100 g) walnut halves

1 carrot, 4 ounces (114 g), quartered

6 large radishes

6-inch (15 cm) zucchini, cut in 1 ½-inch (4 cm) sections

2 (4 ½-ounce/128 g) cooked boneless skinless chicken breasts, each cut in 3 pieces

2 cups (140 g) chopped romaine lettuce

1 cup (240 g) light blue cheese dressing

½ teaspoon kosher salt

¼ teaspoon ground black pepper

8 whole wheat pita pocket halves

1. Place walnuts into the Vitamix container and secure lid.

2. Select Variable 6. Pulse 3 times. Pour into large bowl.

3. Place carrots into the Vitamix container and secure lid.

4. Select Variable 7. Pulse 3 times. Add to walnut mixture.

5. Place radishes and zucchini into the Vitamix container and secure lid.

6. Select Variable 6. Pulse 4 times. Add to bowl.

7. Place chicken into the Vitamix container and secure lid.

8. Select Variable 6. Pulse 3 times. Add to bowl with other ingredients.

9. Add lettuce and dressing to bowl. Add salt and pepper. Toss to mix well. Spoon into pita halves.

Nutritional Information

Amount Per Serving: *Calories 250, Total Fat 11g, Saturated Fat 1.5g, Cholesterol 30mg, Sodium 590mg, Total Carbohydrate 25g, Dietary Fiber 4g, Sugars 4g, Protein 16g*

Make It Your Own

Amp Up Your Sandwich

Instead of using typical burger buns or sliced bread, try new options. Brioche is a rich, pastry-like bread with enough substance to stand in for a bun. Toasted slices from a ciabatta loaf can turn any sandwich into a Panini.

Spelt bread has a nutty, hearty taste. If you're cooking for someone with a gluten intolerance, turn your sandwich into a lettuce wrap by using large-leaf greens such as radicchio, romaine, red lettuce, or collard greens.

If you love wraps, but crave something with more bite, try swapping out your flaxseed wrap with irresistibly chewy naan flatbread.

Butternut Squash Ravioli with Hazelnut Pesto

Preparation: 25 minutes | **Processing:** 1 minute 30 seconds
Cook Time: 10 minutes | **Bake Time:** 30 minutes
Yield: 40 ravioli (8 servings); 1 ¾ cups (420 ml) pesto (14 servings)

Pesto:

1 cup (240 ml) extra virgin olive oil

1 ½ cups (32 g) packed fresh basil leaves

¼ cup (5 g) loosely packed fresh oregano leaves

¾ cup (75 g) grated Parmesan cheese

⅓ cup (52 g) hazelnuts, toasted

2 garlic cloves, peeled

¼ teaspoon ground black pepper

Ravioli:

1 Tablespoon olive oil

4 garlic cloves, peeled

1 small butternut squash, about 1 ¾ pounds (794 g), seeds removed, or 2 cups (410 g) cooked winter squash, any variety

1 cup (100 g) grated Parmesan cheese

4 Tablespoons (57 g) unsalted butter, browned

1 Tablespoon grated nutmeg

2 teaspoons chopped fresh sage

2 teaspoons fresh oregano leaves

Kosher salt, to taste

Ground black pepper, to taste

80 square wonton wrappers

1 large egg, lightly beaten

1. Place all Pesto ingredients into the Vitamix container in the order listed and secure lid.

2. Select Variable 1.

3. Switch machine to Start and slowly increase speed to Variable 6.

4. Blend for 30 seconds. Set aside.

Butternut Squash Ravioli with Hazelnut Pesto *continues on page 290*

Browning Butter

Browned butter is made by cooking butter long enough to turn the milk solids and salt particles brown while cooking out any water present. It adds a rich, nutty, unmistakable flavor to this dish.

Be careful not to burn the butter; stir continuously and maintain a low to medium heat while cooking. Toast the hazelnuts over medium heat in a dry skillet. Toss or stir frequently to prevent burning. Toast until they are a light golden-brown.

It's best to brown butter in a light-colored pan rather than cast iron or a dark-colored pan. This way, you'll be able to easily notice the color change of the butter as it browns.

continued from page 289

Butternut Squash Ravioli with Hazelnut Pesto

5. Heat oven to 450°F (230°C). Rub garlic and squash with 1 Tablespoon olive oil. Wrap garlic in foil and place directly on oven rack. Place squash, cut side down on baking sheet. Bake until tender, 30 minutes. Let cool 15 minutes before scooping out. If using cooked squash, only roast the garlic.

6. Place squash, garlic, Parmesan, butter, nutmeg, sage, oregano, salt, and pepper into the Vitamix container in the order listed and secure lid.

7. Select Variable 1.

8. Switch machine to Start and slowly increase speed to Variable 3.

9. Blend for 20 to 30 seconds, using the tamper to press the ingredients into the blades. Stop machine and remove lid. Scrape down the sides of the container with a spatula and secure lid. Repeat blending process.

10. Place 1 wonton wrapper on a work surface and fill with 1 Tablespoon of ravioli filling. Brush sides with egg and top with another wrapper. Seal edges. Repeat with remaining wrappers and filling.

11. Bring a large pot of salted water to a boil. Working in batches of 8 to 10, add ravioli, and cook until tender, about 2 minutes.

12. Portion onto plates and top with 2 Tablespoons (30 ml) hazelnut pesto.

Nutritional Information

Amount Per Serving (5 ravioli with 2 Tablespoons pesto): *Calories 590, Total Fat 34g, Saturated Fat 10g, Cholesterol 65mg, Sodium 750mg, Total Carbohydrate 54g, Dietary Fiber 4g, Sugars 2g, Protein 17g*

Vegetarian

Pork Tenderloin in Orange-Ginger Sauce

Preparation: 15 minutes | *Processing:* 15–20 seconds | *Cook Time:* 13–15 minutes | *Yield:* 5 servings

1 ¼–1 ½ pounds (568–680 g) pork tenderloin

½ teaspoon salt

¼ teaspoon ground black pepper

1 orange, peeled, halved, plus 1-inch x 2-inch (2.5 cm x 5 cm) strip orange zest

2 thin slices fresh ginger root

1 teaspoon dark sesame oil

1 cup (240 ml) Homemade Chicken Stock (page 163)

2 Tablespoons (30 ml) honey

1 Tablespoon cornstarch

1 Tablespoon vegetable oil

1 small red bell pepper, cut in thin bite-size strips

2 Tablespoons (12 g) sliced green onions

1. Cut tenderloin crosswise into 5 pieces. Place each piece cut side down between pieces of plastic wrap. Pound to ¼-inch (.6 cm) thickness with meat mallet or rolling pin, starting at center. Season with salt and pepper. Set aside.

2. Place orange, ginger, sesame oil, chicken stock, honey, and cornstarch into the Vitamix container and secure lid.

3. Select Variable 1.

4. Switch machine to Start and slowly increase speed to Variable 7. Blend for 15 to 20 seconds.

5. Heat oil in 12-inch (30 cm) nonstick skillet over medium-high heat. Add pork. Cook 8 to 10 minutes or until deep golden-brown, turning once. Remove from skillet; add bell pepper. Cook 2 minutes. Return pork to skillet. Pour orange mixture into skillet. Cook 3 minutes, stirring occasionally until pork is no longer pink and sauce is bubbly and thickened. Serve sauce over pork. Sprinkle with green onions.

Nutritional Information

Amount Per Serving: Calories 210, Total Fat 6g, Saturated Fat 1.5g, Cholesterol 80mg, Sodium 300mg, Total Carbohydrate 13g, Dietary Fiber 1g, Sugars 10g, Protein 26g

Dairy-free

Coconut Fish Curry

Preparation: 30 minutes | **Processing:** Pulsing | **Cook Time:** 15 minutes | **Yield:** 4 servings

2 ounces (56 g) shallots, halved

9 ½ ounce (270 g) red bell pepper, cut into 2-inch (5 cm) pieces

½-inch (1.3 cm) cube fresh ginger root

1 Tablespoon vegetable oil

2 ½ teaspoons Thai red curry paste

1 (14 ounce/414 ml) can light coconut milk

1 Tablespoon fish sauce

zest of 2 limes

2 Tablespoons (30 ml) fresh lime juice

1 pound (454 g) halibut fillets, cut into 1 ½-inch (4 cm) chunks

½ pound (227 g) peeled, deveined, and uncooked shrimp

Salt and ground black pepper, to taste

⅓ cup (5 g) chopped fresh cilantro leaves

⅓ cup (8 g) chopped fresh basil leaves

2 cups (300 g) cooked brown rice

1. Place shallots, bell pepper, and ginger into the Vitamix container and secure lid.

2. Select Variable 5.

3. Pulse 3 times. Stop machine and remove lid. Scrape down the sides of the container with a spatula and secure lid. Pulse 2 more times.

4. Heat oil in a large saucepan over medium-high heat. Add chopped shallots, bell pepper, and ginger. Sauté until peppers are softened, about 5 minutes. Stir in curry paste, coconut milk, fish sauce, lime zest, and lime juice. Simmer gently, stirring often, about 5 minutes.

5. Add fish and shrimp to sauce. Return to a simmer and cook until fish and shrimp are opaque in the center, about 5 to 6 minutes. Season to taste with salt and pepper. Stir in cilantro and basil.

6. Serve over rice.

Nutritional Information

Amount Per Serving (with ½ cup (75 g) cooked rice): *Calories 400, Total Fat 13g, Saturated Fat 7g, Cholesterol 125mg, Sodium 850mg, Total Carbohydrate 38g, Dietary Fiber 4g, Sugars 4g, Protein 32g*

Dairy-free

Coconut Curry Chicken

Preparation: 20 minutes | **Processing:** 3 minutes 10 seconds | **Cook Time:** 10 minutes
Bake Time: 1 hour 30 minutes | **Yield:** 4 servings

¼ cup (65 g) peanut butter

1 (14-ounce / 400 ml) can light coconut milk

⅓ cup (80 ml) Homemade Chicken Stock (page 163)

2 Tablespoons (30 ml) reduced sodium soy sauce

2 Tablespoons (30 ml) rice vinegar

1 Tablespoon packed brown sugar

1 Tablespoon toasted sesame oil

2 teaspoons red curry paste

1 teaspoon chopped fresh ginger root

1 garlic clove, peeled

⅛ – ¼ teaspoon cayenne pepper

½ cup (63 g) all-purpose flour

½ teaspoon salt

½ teaspoon ground black pepper

3 pounds (1.4 kg) chicken bone-in parts (legs, thighs, breasts)

2 Tablespoons (30 ml) vegetable oil

2 Tablespoons (2 g) chopped fresh cilantro leaves

2 cups (316 g) cooked brown rice

1. Place peanut butter, coconut milk, chicken stock, soy sauce, vinegar, brown sugar, sesame oil, red curry paste, ginger, garlic, and cayenne pepper into the Vitamix container and secure lid.

2. Select Variable 1.

3. Switch machine to Start and slowly increase speed to Variable 5.

4. Blend for 10 seconds. Stop machine and remove lid.

5. Scrape down the sides of the container with a spatula and secure lid. Switch machine to Start and blend an additional 3 minutes. Set aside.

6. Preheat oven to 300°F (150°C).

7. In a plastic bag, combine flour, salt, and black pepper. Add chicken pieces to flour mixture, shaking to coat.

Coconut Curry Chicken continues on page 294

continued from page 293

Coconut Curry Chicken

8. In a large skillet, cook chicken in hot oil until browned. Transfer to an ungreased rectangular baking dish. Pour sauce over chicken, cover with foil, and bake for 1 hour. Uncover and bake an additional 20 to 30 minutes, until chicken is very tender.

9. Transfer to a serving platter. Spoon sauce over chicken, sprinkle with cilantro, and serve over cooked rice.

Nutritional Information

Amount Per Serving (with ¼ Cup (60 ml) Sauce): *Calories 470, Total Fat 15g, Saturated Fat 3.5g, Cholesterol 150mg, Sodium 580mg, Total Carbohydrate 29g, Dietary Fiber 2g, Sugars 1g, Protein 53g*

Dairy-free

Thai Pork Satay

Preparation: 20 minutes | **Processing:** 35 seconds
Cook Time: 7 minutes | **Chill Time:** 4 hours
Yield: 20 skewers (10 servings)

2 cups (480 ml) light coconut milk, divided use

1 ounce (28 g) lemongrass

¼ cup (60 ml) coconut oil

2 Tablespoons (18 g) chopped fresh ginger root

2 Tablespoons (28 g) dark brown sugar

1 Tablespoon ground turmeric

1 Tablespoon ground coriander

2 teaspoons kosher salt

1 teaspoon ground cumin

¼ teaspoon cayenne pepper

1 ½ pounds (680 g) pork loin, cut into 1-inch x ¼-inch (2.5 cm x .6 cm) slices

20 wooden skewers, soaked in water for 30 minutes

1. Place 1 cup (240 ml) coconut milk, lemongrass, oil, ginger, sugar, turmeric, coriander, salt, cumin, and cayenne pepper into the Vitamix container in the order listed and secure lid.

2. Select Variable 1.

3. Switch machine to Start and slowly increase speed to Variable 7.

4. Blend for 20 seconds. Stop the machine and remove lid. Scrape down the sides of the container with a spatula and secure lid. Switch machine to Start and blend an additional 15 seconds.

5. Toss pork with sauce in a bowl; chill 4 hours.

6. Pour remaining 1 cup (240 ml) coconut milk into a bowl. Thread 3 slices of pork onto each skewer, dip into coconut milk, and grill until lightly charred, about 7 minutes.

Nutritional Information

Amount Per Serving: *Calories 200, Total Fat 14g, Saturated Fat 10g, Cholesterol 35mg, Sodium 640mg, Total Carbohydrate 6g, Dietary Fiber 0g, Sugars 3g, Protein 13g*

Dairy-free

Gluten-free

World Cuisine

Thrill of the Grill

Satay is a Southeast Asian dish consisting of seasoned, skewered and grilled meat, served with a sauce (typically peanut sauce). There are many variations of satay that have been adapted by different regions based on the meat and ingredients used and the method of cooking.

Vegetarians can still enjoy this dish by replacing meat with tofu. Because satay is seasoned with a variety of spices, tofu works as an excellent substitute due to its flavor-absorbing qualities.

To make it a full meal, serve satay with peanut noodles or your choice of grilled or sautéed vegetables.

Indian Vegetable Stew

Preparation: 20 minutes | **Processing:** 10–15 seconds
Cook Time: 40 minutes | **Yield:** 4 servings

1-inch (2.5 cm) cube fresh ginger root

2 garlic cloves, peeled

1 (15-ounce/425 g) can unsalted diced tomatoes

½ teaspoon cayenne pepper

1 medium onion, 4 ounces (114 g), chopped

½ large yellow bell pepper, 4 ½ ounces (128 g), diced

1 cup (240 ml) water, divided use

8 ounces (227 g) boiling potatoes, peeled and cubed

2 medium carrots, 5 ounces (142 g), sliced

1 ½ teaspoons garam masala

½ teaspoon chili powder

3 cups (300 g) chopped cauliflower florets (¾ pound)

½ cup (120 ml) light coconut milk

Sea salt, to taste

Ground black pepper, to taste

1. Place ginger, garlic, tomatoes, and cayenne into the Vitamix container and secure lid. Select Variable 1.

2. Switch machine to Start and slowly increase speed to Variable 5. Blend for 10 to 15 seconds. Set aside.

3. Preheat a saucepan over medium-low heat. Add onion and bell pepper and a few Tablespoons of water. Sauté 10 minutes, or until softened, stirring frequently. Continue to add water, a few Tablespoons at a time, as needed to prevent the vegetables from sticking.

4. Stir in potatoes, carrots, garam masala, and chili powder. Cover and cook over medium-low heat for 10 minutes, stirring occasionally. Continue adding a few Tablespoons of water as it evaporates.

5. Add cauliflower, tomato mixture and ½ cup (120 ml) water. Cover and simmer 20 minutes. Remove from heat and stir in coconut milk. Season to taste with salt and black pepper.

Nutritional Information

Amount Per Serving: *Calories 140, Total Fat 2.5g, Saturated Fat 2g, Cholesterol 0mg, Sodium 85mg, Total Carbohydrate 27g, Dietary Fiber 5g, Sugars 9g, Protein 5g*

Vegan   **Vegetarian**   **Dairy-free**   **Gluten-free**

Desserts

Vegan

Vegetarian

Dairy-free

Gluten-free

Now it's easier than ever to create enticing, guilt-free desserts. In addition to fresh fruit sorbets, enjoy delectable treats such as Mini Almond Macaroons and Low-Fat Pumpkin Pie.

Desserts

MILKSHAKES / FROZEN DESSERTS / BAKED DESSERTS / DESSERT CONDIMENTS

Banana Cream Pie Milkshake

Preparation: 10 minutes | **Processing:** 40 seconds
Yield: 4 cups (960 ml) (4 servings)

¼ cup (60 ml) plus 2 Tablespoons
(30 ml) skim milk

3 cups (400 g) nonfat vanilla Greek frozen yogurt

1 banana, peeled and cut into large chunks

¼ cup (21 g) plus 2 Tablespoons (11 g)
graham cracker crumbs

1. Place all ingredients into the Vitamix container in the order listed and secure lid.

2. Select Variable 1.

3. Switch machine to Start and slowly increase speed to Variable 8.

4. Blend for 40 seconds or until desired consistency is reached, using the tamper to press the ingredients into the blades.

Nutritional Information

Amount Per Serving: Calories 220, Total Fat 1g, Saturated Fat 0g, Cholesterol 10mg, Sodium 150mg, Total Carbohydrate 39g, Dietary Fiber 1g, Sugars 36g, Protein 11g

Vegetarian

Chef's Note

Greek yogurt makes this milkshake a filling and satisfying snack or a decadent, guilt-free dessert. Since Greek yogurt has more protein, less sodium, and fewer carbohydrates than regular yogurt, it will help you feel fuller longer, while eliminating unnecessary fat and calories.

Old-Fashioned
Vanilla Milkshake

Preparation: 10 minutes | **Processing:** 15 seconds | **Yield:** 4 ¾ cups (1.1 l) (4 servings)

1 ¾ cups (420 ml) milk

4 cups (520 g) vanilla ice cream

2 ½ teaspoons vanilla extract

1. Place all ingredients into the Vitamix container in the order listed and secure lid.

2. Select Variable 1.

3. Switch machine to Start and slowly increase speed to Variable 8.

4. Blend for 15 seconds or until desired consistency is reached.

Nutritional Information

Amount Per Serving: *Calories 340, Total Fat 18g, Saturated Fat 10g, Cholesterol 50mg, Sodium 115mg, Total Carbohydrate 36g, Dietary Fiber 0g, Sugars 34g, Protein 10g*

Vegetarian **Gluten-free**

Strawberry White Chocolate Milkshake

Preparation: 10 minutes | ***Processing:*** 1 minute | ***Yield:*** 4 ½ cups (1.0 l) (4 servings)

1 cup (240 ml) skim milk

2 cups (268 g) nonfat vanilla Greek frozen yogurt

½ cup (120 g) white chocolate chips

2 cups (300 g) frozen unsweetened strawberries

1. Place all ingredients into the Vitamix container in the order listed and secure lid.

2. Select Variable 1.

3. Switch machine to Start and slowly increase speed to Variable 10.

4. Blend for 1 minute or until desired consistency is reached, using the tamper to press the ingredients into the blades.

Nutritional Information

Amount Per Serving: *Calories 280, Total Fat 8g, Saturated Fat 7g, Cholesterol 5mg, Sodium 120mg, Total Carbohydrate 45g, Dietary Fiber 2g, Sugars 39g, Protein 9g*

Vegetarian

Mocha Shake

Preparation: 20 minutes | **Processing:** 20–25 seconds
Yield: 4 cups (960 ml) (4 servings)

½ cup (120 ml) cold coffee

2 Tablespoons (30 ml) chocolate syrup

4 cups (528 g) vanilla ice cream

1 cup (240 ml) ice cubes

1. Place all ingredients into the Vitamix container in the order listed and secure lid.

2. Select Variable 1.

3. Switch machine to Start and slowly increase speed to Variable 8.

4. Blend for 20 to 25 seconds or until desired consistency is reached, using the tamper to press the ingredients into the blades.

Nutritional Information

Amount Per Serving: *Calories 330, Total Fat 18g, Saturated Fat 10g, Cholesterol 50mg, Sodium 80mg, Total Carbohydrate 36g, Dietary Fiber 0g, Sugars 33g, Protein 6g*

Vegetarian   Gluten-free

Maple Nut Milkshake

Preparation: 10 minutes | **Processing:** 30 seconds
Yield: 3 ½ cups (840 ml) (3 servings)

3 cups (408 g) nonfat vanilla Greek frozen yogurt

¼ cup (60 ml) plus 2 Tablespoons (30 ml) skim milk

1 ½ teaspoons vanilla extract

3 Tablespoons (45 ml) maple syrup

¼ cup (25 g) walnuts

1. Place all ingredients into the Vitamix container in the order listed and secure lid.

2. Select Variable 1.

3. Switch machine to Start and slowly increase speed to Variable 8.

4. Blend for 30 seconds or until desired consistency is reached, using the tamper to press the ingredients into the blades.

Nutritional Information

Amount Per Serving: *Calories 330, Total Fat 6g, Saturated Fat 0.5g, Cholesterol 10mg, Sodium 150mg, Total Carbohydrate 51g, Dietary Fiber 1g, Sugars 53g, Protein 15g*

Vegetarian

Create Your Own

Milkshakes After Five

A milkshake can easily become a fun frozen cocktail. Try a small amount of chocolate, vanilla, or coffee-flavored liqueur in your favorite milkshake recipes. For a more spirited addition, try rum to deepen the flavor of the Maple Nut and Pineapple Shakes, while bourbon livens up the Old-Fashioned Vanilla and Banana Cream Pie Milkshakes.

Be sure to stir in only a tablespoon or two of alcohol as too much will overpower the flavors and prevent the drink from freezing properly.

Chocolate Shake

Preparation: 10 minutes | **Processing:** 20 seconds | **Yield:** 2 cups (480 ml) (2 servings)

¼ cup (60 ml) milk

¼ cup (60 ml) chocolate syrup

3 cups (414 g) chocolate ice cream

1. Place all ingredients into the Vitamix container in the order listed and secure lid.

2. Select Variable 1.

3. Switch machine to Start and slowly increase speed to Variable 10.

4. Blend for 20 seconds or until desired consistency is reached, using the tamper to press the ingredients into the blades.

Nutritional Information

Amount Per Serving: Calories 570, Total Fat 25g, Saturated Fat 16g, Cholesterol 65mg, Sodium 135mg, Total Carbohydrate 76g, Dietary Fiber 4g, Sugars 69g, Protein 11g

Vegetarian   Gluten-free

Pineapple Milkshake

Preparation: 10 minutes | ***Processing:*** 30 seconds | ***Yield:*** 4 cups (960 ml) (4 servings)

1 cup (240 ml) pineapple juice

1 cup (240 ml) skim milk

2 ½ cups (330 g) vanilla ice cream

2 cups (374 g) frozen unsweetened pineapple
chunks, partially thawed

½ teaspoon ground cinnamon

1. Place all ingredients into the Vitamix container in the order
   listed and secure lid.

2. Select Variable 1.

3. Switch machine to Start and slowly increase speed to Variable 8,
   using the tamper to press the ingredients into the blades.

4. Blend for 30 seconds or until desired consistency is reached.

Nutritional Information

Amount Per Serving: *Calories 290, Total Fat 11g, Saturated Fat 6g, Cholesterol 30mg,
Sodium 70mg, Total Carbohydrate 42g, Dietary Fiber 2g, Sugars 29g, Protein 6g*

Vegetarian   **Gluten-free**

Peachy Buttermilk Milkshake

Preparation: 15 minutes | **Processing:** 20 seconds | **Yield:** 4 ½ cups (1.0 l) (4 servings)

2 cups (480 ml) low-fat buttermilk

⅛ teaspoon almond extract

2 cups (280 g) frozen unsweetened peach slices

2 cups (264 g) vanilla ice cream, softened

1. Place all ingredients into the Vitamix container in the order listed and secure lid.

2. Select Variable 1.

3. Switch machine to Start and slowly increase speed to Variable 10.

4. Blend for 20 seconds or until desired consistency is reached.

Nutritional Information

Amount Per Serving: *Calories 230, Total Fat 10g, Saturated Fat 6g, Cholesterol 35mg, Sodium 170mg, Total Carbohydrate 29g, Dietary Fiber 1g, Sugars 26g, Protein 8g*

Vegetarian **Gluten-free**

Tropical Shake

Preparation: 15 minutes | *Processing:* 40 seconds | *Yield:* 3 ¼ cups (780 ml) (3 servings)

1 cup (240 ml) pineapple juice

¾ cup (180 ml) unsweetened plain soy milk

½ lemon, peeled

1 banana, peeled and frozen

1 cup (187 g) frozen unsweetened mango chunks

1. Place all ingredients into the Vitamix container in the order listed and secure lid.

2. Select Variable 1.

3. Switch machine to Start and slowly increase speed to Variable 8.

4. Blend for 40 seconds or until desired consistency is reached.

Nutritional Information

Amount Per Serving: Calories 150, Total Fat 1.5g, Saturated Fat 0g, Cholesterol 0mg, Sodium 5mg, Total Carbohydrate 32g, Dietary Fiber 3g, Sugars 23g, Protein 4g

Vegan   **Vegetarian**   **Dairy-free**   **Gluten-free**

Orange Sorbet

Preparation: 10 minutes | **Processing:** 30 seconds
Yield: 3 cups (720 ml) (6 servings)

2 large oranges, peeled and halved

1 Tablespoon orange juice concentrate

1 teaspoon orange zest

2 Tablespoons (30 ml) honey

4 cups (960 ml) ice cubes

1. Place all ingredients into the Vitamix container in the order listed and secure lid.

2. Select Variable 1.

3. Switch machine to Start and slowly increase speed to Variable 10. Use the tamper to press the ingredients into the blades.

4. In about 30 seconds, the sound of the motor will change and four mounds should form.

5. Stop machine. Do not overmix or melting will occur. Serve immediately.

Nutritional Information

Amount Per Serving: *Calories 50, Saturated Fat 0g, Cholesterol 0mg, Sodium 0mg, Total Carbohydrate 12g, Dietary Fiber 1g, Sugars 10g, Protein 0g*

Vegetarian **Dairy-free** **Gluten-free**

Chef's Note

Serve each scoop of Orange Sorbet in a hollowed-out orange half and top with orange zest, a drizzle of honey, or sprinkling of grated dark chocolate.

Peach Soy Sherbet

Preparation: 10 minutes | **Processing:** 45 seconds
Yield: 5 cups (1.2 l) (10 servings)

1 ½ cups (360 ml) plain unsweetened soy yogurt

3 Tablespoons (45 ml) honey

1 teaspoon vanilla extract

1 ½ pounds (680 g) frozen unsweetened peach slices

1. Place all ingredients into the Vitamix container in the order listed and secure lid.

2. Select Variable 1.

3. Switch machine to Start and slowly increase speed to Variable 10. Use the tamper to press the ingredients into the blades.

4. In about 45 seconds, the sound of the motor will change and four mounds should form.

5. Stop machine. Do not overmix or melting will occur. Serve immediately.

Nutritional Information

Amount Per Serving: *Calories 70, Total Fat 1g, Saturated Fat 0g, Cholesterol 0mg, Sodium 0mg, Total Carbohydrate 13g, Dietary Fiber 1g, Sugars 11g, Protein 2g*

Vegetarian   **Dairy-free**   **Gluten-free**

Chef's Note

Soy yogurt *is a mixture of ground soy beans and water, with nutrition profiles similar to cow's milk. Purchase unsweetened, unflavored soy milk for this recipe or blend homemade Soy Milk (see Beverages).*

Mixed Spice Berry Sorbet

Preparation: 15 minutes | **Processing:** 1 minute 15 seconds
Yield: 4 ¼ cups (1.0 l) (9 servings)

½ ounce (14 g) fresh ginger
root, peeled

1 cup (240 ml) cold water

½ cup (100 g) pitted dates

1 cup (150 g) frozen
unsweetened strawberries

1 cup (140 g) frozen
unsweetened blueberries

1 cup (140 g) frozen
unsweetened blackberries

1 cup (140 g) frozen
unsweetened red raspberries

2 cups (300 g) frozen pitted
Bing cherries

½ cup (13 g) fresh mint leaves

⅛ teaspoon ground cloves

⅛ teaspoon ground allspice

¼ teaspoon ground nutmeg

½ teaspoon ground cinnamon

1 teaspoon vanilla extract

1. Partially thaw frozen berries for 10 minutes; set aside.

2. Place ginger, water, and dates into the Vitamix container in the order listed and secure lid. Select Variable 1.

3. Switch machine to Start and slowly increase speed to Variable 10.

4. Blend for 30 seconds until ginger and dates are finely chopped. Stop machine and remove lid. Add berries, mint, cloves, allspice, nutmeg, cinnamon, and vanilla to the container with ginger mixture and secure lid. Select Variable 1.

5. Switch machine to Start and slowly increase speed to Variable 10. Use the tamper to press the ingredients into the blades. In about 45 to 55 seconds, the sound of the motor will change and four mounds should form.

6. Stop machine. Do not overmix or melting will occur. Serve immediately.

Nutritional Information

Amount Per Serving: *Calories 80, Total Fat 0g, Saturated Fat 0g, Cholesterol 0mg, Sodium 0mg, Total Carbohydrate 20g, Dietary Fiber 4g, Sugars 15g, Protein 1g*

Vegan   **Vegetarian**   **Dairy-free**   **Gluten-free**

Strawberry Grand Marnier Sorbet

Preparation: 10 minutes | **Processing:** 45–55 seconds | **Yield:** 3 cups (720 ml) (6 servings)

1 cup (240 ml) orange juice

4 ounces (120 ml) Grand Marnier

½ pound (227 g) frozen unsweetened pineapple chunks

1 ½ pounds (680 g) frozen unsweetened strawberries

1. Place all ingredients into the Vitamix container in the order listed and secure lid.

2. Select Variable 1.

3. Switch machine to Start and slowly increase speed to Variable 10. Use the tamper to press the ingredients into the blades.

4. In about 45 to 55 seconds, the sound of the motor will change and four mounds should form.

5. Stop machine. Do not overmix or melting will occur. Serve immediately.

Nutritional Information

Amount Per Serving: *Calories 70, Total Fat 0g, Saturated Fat 0g, Cholesterol 0mg, Sodium 0mg, Total Carbohydrate 12g, Dietary Fiber 2g, Sugars 10g, Protein 1g*

Vegan **Vegetarian** **Dairy-free** **Gluten-free**

Strawberry Freeze

Preparation: 10 minutes | **Processing:** 30 seconds
Yield: 5 cups (1.2 l) (10 servings)

1 ½ cups (360 ml) unsweetened almond milk

3 Tablespoons (45 ml) honey

1 ½ pounds (680 g) frozen unsweetened strawberries

1. Place all ingredients into the Vitamix container in the order
   listed and secure lid.

2. Select Variable 1.

3. Switch machine to Start and slowly increase speed to Variable 10.
   Use the tamper to press the ingredients into the blades.

4. In about 30 seconds, the sound of the motor will change
   and four mounds should form.

5. Stop machine. Do not overmix or melting will occur.

6. Stir in any honey that may be on top. Serve immediately.

Nutritional Information

Amount Per Serving: *Calories 50, Total Fat 0g, Saturated Fat 0g, Cholesterol 0mg,
Sodium 25mg, Total Carbohydrate 12g, Dietary Fiber 2g, Sugars 8g, Protein 1g*

Vegetarian   **Dairy-free**   **Gluten-free**

Chef's Note

Try swapping out *the
strawberries for blueberries,
blackberries, or even a
peach-mango combination.
If substituting small berries
for strawberries, you will
need to increase the
amount called for.*

Mixed Fruit and Chocolate Freeze

Preparation: 10 minutes | **Processing:** 45–55 seconds | **Yield:** 4 cups (960 ml) (8 servings)

1 ½ cups (360 ml) low-fat vanilla
or plain yogurt

1 cup (147 g) coarsely chopped dark chocolate

1 ½ teaspoons vanilla extract

1 ½ pounds (680 g) frozen unsweetened fruit,
half strawberries and half mango chunks, softened
for 5 minutes

1. Place all ingredients into the Vitamix container in the order listed and secure lid.

2. Select Variable 1.

3. Switch machine to Start and slowly increase speed to Variable 10. Use the tamper to press the ingredients into the blades.

4. In about 45 to 55 seconds, the sound of the motor will change and four mounds should form.

5. Stop machine. Do not overmix or melting will occur. Serve immediately.

Nutritional Information

Amount Per Serving: *Calories 190, Total Fat 8g, Saturated Fat 5g, Cholesterol 5mg, Sodium 35mg, Total Carbohydrate 26g, Dietary Fiber 4g, Sugars 19g, Protein 4g*

Vegetarian **Gluten-free**

Herbed Apple Granita

Preparation: 10 minutes plus overnight freezing
Processing: 40 seconds–1 minute | **Yield:** 4 cups (960 ml) (8 servings)

3 cups (720 ml) apple juice

4 teaspoons fresh lemon juice

½ cup (120 ml) honey

½ cup (48 g) fresh tarragon leaves

1. Place all ingredients into the Vitamix container in the order listed and secure lid.

2. Select Variable 1.

3. Switch machine to Start and slowly increase speed to Variable 10.

4. Blend for 20 to 30 seconds.

5. Pour into two standard ice cube trays and freeze overnight. Let trays thaw at room temperature for 10 minutes.

6. Place ice cubes into the Vitamix container and secure lid.

7. Select Variable 1.

8. Switch machine to Start and slowly increase speed to Variable 10.

9. Blend for 20 to 30 seconds, using the tamper to press the ice cubes into the blades. As mixture begins to freeze, the sound of the motor will change and the mixture will start to flow freely through the blades. Toward the end of processing, leave the tamper inserted through the lid plug opening to encourage the formation of four mounds.

Nutritional Information

Amount Per Serving: Calories 110, Total Fat 0g, Saturated Fat 0g, Cholesterol 0mg, Sodium 10mg, Total Carbohydrate 28g, Dietary Fiber 0g, Sugars 26g, Protein 0g

Vegetarian   **Dairy-free**   **Gluten-free**

Vegan Raisin Almond Cookies

Preparation: 20 minutes | **Processing:** 30 seconds
Bake Time: 14 minutes | **Yield:** 44 cookies

¾ cup (180 ml) cold, strong coffee

¼ cup (56 g) vegan margarine, melted and cooled

1 teaspoon almond extract

½ cup (80 g) pitted prunes

1 ⅓ cups (267 g) granulated sugar

1 Tablespoon flaxseed

2 ¼ cups (280 g) all-purpose flour

¾ teaspoon baking powder

¾ teaspoon baking soda

¼ teaspoon salt

¾ cup (120 g) golden raisins

½ cup (72 g) chopped almonds

Chef's Note

It's easy to *dress up these buttery tasting almond cookies for a special occasion. Press a roasted almond into the center of each cookie after removing from the oven.*

1. Line a baking sheet with silpat or parchment paper. Preheat oven to 375°F (190°C).

2. Place coffee, melted margarine, almond extract, prunes, sugar, and flaxseed into the Vitamix container in the order listed and secure lid. Select Variable 1.

3. Switch machine to Start and slowly increase speed to Variable 10.

4. Blend for 30 seconds.

5. Place flour, baking powder, baking soda, and salt into a medium-size mixing bowl. Stir by hand to combine.

6. Pour wet mixture into dry ingredients and stir by hand to combine. Stir in raisins and almonds.

7. Drop by rounded Tablespoons onto prepared baking sheet.

8. Bake for 14 minutes. Transfer to a wire rack to cool.

Nutritional Information

Amount Per Cookie: *Calories 80, Total Fat 2g, Saturated Fat 0g, Cholesterol 0mg, Sodium 65mg, Total Carbohydrate 15g, Dietary Fiber 1g, Sugars 9g, Protein 1g*

Vegan

Vegetarian

Dairy-free

Mini Almond Macaroons

Preparation: 10 minutes | ***Processing:*** Pulsing
Bake Time: 12–15 minutes | ***Yield:*** 25 small macaroons

6 ounces (170 g) almond paste

6 Tablespoons (75 g) plus
2 teaspoons granulated sugar

2 large egg whites

1. Line a baking sheet with parchment paper. Preheat oven to 325°F (160°C).

2. Place almond paste and sugar into the Vitamix container and secure lid.

3. Select Variable 7.

4. Pulse 10 times to combine. Add egg white. Pulse an additional 10 times.
   Stop and scrape down the sides of the container with a spatula. Secure lid
   and continue to Pulse until blended.

5. Place batter in a medium-size pastry bag fitted with a small round tip.

6. Pipe batter into small circles on prepared baking sheet.

7. Bake 12 to 15 minutes until they begin to brown on the edges.
   Cool and then loosen with a spatula.

Nutritional Information

Amount Per Macaroon: *Calories 50, Total Fat 1.5g, Saturated Fat 0g, Cholesterol 0mg,
Sodium 0mg, Total Carbohydrate 7g, Dietary Fiber 0g, Sugars 6g, Protein 1g*

Vegetarian **Dairy-free** **Gluten-free**

Raisin Almond Cheesecake

Preparation: 20 minutes | *Processing:* Pulsing plus 20 seconds
Bake Time: 60 minutes | *Yield:* 12 servings

Crust:

¾ cup (94 g) all-purpose flour

2 Tablespoons (25 g)
granulated sugar

⅛ teaspoon salt

⅓ cup (75 g) unsalted butter

Filling:

2 ½ cups (620 g) ricotta cheese

½ cup (100 g) granulated sugar

3 Tablespoons (23 g) all-purpose flour

3 large eggs

1 Tablespoon orange zest

1 teaspoon vanilla extract

¼ teaspoon salt

2 Tablespoons (20 g) golden raisins
or chopped, dried cherries

1 Tablespoon lemon zest

2 Tablespoons (18 g)
chopped almonds

1. Preheat oven to 475°F (250°C). Spray the bottom of a 9-inch (23 cm)
   spring-form pan well with cooking spray.

2. Place flour, sugar, salt, and butter into the Vitamix container in the order listed and secure lid.
   Select Variable 6. Pulse 4 times until coarsely combined. Press mixture into the bottom of spring-form pan.

3. Bake for 10 minutes or until light-golden on top. Cool on wire rack. Reduce heat to 350°F (180°C).

4. Place ricotta cheese, sugar, flour, eggs, orange zest, vanilla, and salt into the Vitamix container
   in the order listed and secure lid. Select Variable 3. Switch machine to Start and blend for 15 seconds.
   Stop the machine, remove the lid, and scrape down the sides of the container with a spatula.
   Secure lid and blend an additional 5 seconds.

5. Pour into a bowl. Stir in raisins, lemon zest, and almonds. Pour mixture over crust.
   Bake for 50 minutes or until center is set.

6. Run a knife around edge of cheesecake to loosen. Let cool completely on a wire rack. Cover and chill 8 hours.

Nutritional Information

Amount Per Serving: Calories 210, Total Fat 14g, Saturated Fat 8g, Cholesterol 85mg,
Sodium 135mg, Total Carbohydrate 13g, Dietary Fiber 1g, Sugars 4g, Protein 9g

Vegetarian

Brown Sugar Surprise Cupcakes

Preparation: 20 minutes | **Processing:** 30 seconds | **Bake Time:** 20–25 minutes | **Yield:** 24 full-size cupcakes

1 ¼ cups (300 ml) milk

2 large eggs

1 ½ teaspoons vanilla extract

⅔ cup (150 g) unsalted butter, softened

1 ¾ cups (350 g) granulated sugar

2 ½ cups (312 g) all-purpose flour

2 ½ teaspoons baking powder

½ teaspoon salt

½ cup (110 g) packed brown sugar

¼ cup (27 g) finely chopped pecans

1 teaspoon ground cinnamon

Creamy Butter Frosting (page 335)

1. Line 24 (2 ½-inch/6 cm) muffin cups with paper baking cups. Preheat oven to 350°F (180°C).

2. Place milk, eggs, vanilla, butter, and sugar into the Vitamix container in the order listed and secure lid. Select Variable 1.

3. Switch machine to Start and slowly increase speed to Variable 7. Blend for 30 seconds.

4. In a large-size mixing bowl, combine flour, baking powder, and salt.

5. Pour wet mixture into dry ingredients and stir by hand to combine.

6. In a small bowl, whisk together brown sugar, pecans, and cinnamon.

7. Spoon 1 Tablespoon of batter into each prepared muffin cup. Sprinkle 1 teaspoon of the brown sugar mixture on top of the batter. Repeat layers by spooning remaining batter evenly between cups, and sprinkle remaining brown sugar mixture on top.

8. Bake for 20 to 25 minutes, or until a toothpick inserted into the center comes out clean. Cool on wire racks for 10 minutes. Remove cupcakes from muffin cups and cool completely. Top each cupcake with 2 Tablespoons (30 g) Creamy Butter Frosting.

Nutritional Information

Amount Per Cupcake: *Calories 190, Total Fat 7g, Saturated Fat 3.5g, Cholesterol 30mg, Sodium 115mg, Total Carbohydrate 30g, Dietary Fiber 1g, Sugars 20 g, Protein 2g*

Vegetarian

Low-Fat Pumpkin Pie

Preparation: 15 minutes | **Processing:** 10–15 seconds
Bake Time: 55 minutes | **Yield:** 3 pies (24 slices)

1 cup (240 ml) egg substitute

3 ½ cups (850 g)
canned pumpkin

1 ½ cups (300 g)
granulated sugar

1 teaspoon salt

2 teaspoons ground cinnamon

1 teaspoon ground ginger

½ teaspoon ground cloves

3 cups (720 ml) evaporated
nonfat milk

3 unbaked 9-inch (23 cm)
deep dish pie shells

Whipped topping (optional)

1. Preheat oven to 425°F (220°C).

2. Place egg substitute, pumpkin, sugar, salt, cinnamon, ginger, cloves, and evaporated milk into the Vitamix container in the order listed and secure lid.

3. Select Variable 1.

4. Switch machine to Start and slowly increase speed to Variable 5.

5. Blend for 10 to 15 seconds.

6. Pour into pie shells.

7. Bake for 15 minutes. Reduce oven temperature to 350°F (180°C). Bake for 40 minutes. Pie is done when a knife inserted into the center comes out clean. Filling will be soft, but firms up as it sets and cools.

8. Chill and serve topped with whipped topping.

Nutritional Information

Amount Per Slice: *Calories 220, Total Fat 8g, Saturated Fat 2.5g, Cholesterol 0mg, Sodium 250mg, Total Carbohydrate 32g, Dietary Fiber 2g, Sugars 17g, Protein 5g*

Vegetarian

Pumpkin Purée

Some of the best-tasting dishes use all-natural, homemade ingredients. It's easy to create your own pumpkin purée to use in pies, smoothies, and more.

Start with a small-size pie pumpkin. Cut off the stem and cut the pumpkin in half. Scoop out the seeds and stringy insides. (You can save the seeds for roasting, if you'd like.) Cut the pumpkin into wedges about the size of your hand.

Preheat an oven to 350°F (180°C) and place the pumpkin wedges either face up or face down on a baking sheet. Allow the pumpkin to bake for about 45 minutes or until the pumpkin is fork-tender. Carefully remove the pumpkin skin. It should peel off effortlessly. Once all the skin has been removed, blend the remaining pumpkin until puréed. If the purée is too dry, simply add a little water to moisten the mixture.

Vanilla Custard Sauce

Preparation: 10 minutes | ***Processing:*** 5 minutes
Yield: 4 ½ cups (1.0 l) (18 Servings)

6 large egg yolks

1 ½ cups (360 ml) half & half

¼ cup (30 g) all-purpose flour

½ cup (100 g) granulated sugar

⅛ teaspoon salt

1 Tablespoon unsalted butter

1 Tablespoon vanilla extract

1. Place all ingredients into the Vitamix container in the order listed and secure lid.

2. Select Variable 1.

3. Switch machine to Start and slowly increase speed to Variable 10.

4. Blend for 5 minutes or until steam escapes from the vented lid.

Nutritional Information

Amount Per Serving: *Calories 80, Total Fat 4.5g, Saturated Fat 2.5g, Cholesterol 70mg, Sodium 35mg, Total Carbohydrate 8g, Dietary Fiber 0g, Sugars 6g, Protein 2g*

Looking Good

Razzle and Dazzle

You can turn an ordinary dessert into an extraordinary work of culinary art simply by adding a drizzle, a swirl, or a swoosh of colorful syrup or sauce.

Drizzle Fresh Fruit Syrup (see Breakfasts) over the Whipped Cream (see Desserts) garnish of any dessert just before serving. Swirl Mixed Berry Purée (see Page 332) or chocolate sauce on white plates before adding a piece of cake or pie; swirl Vanilla Custard Sauce on dark plates for contrast. Use a toothpick to draw patterns in the sauce for a decorative effect.

Mixed Berry Purée

Preparation: 10 minutes | **Processing:** 3 minutes
Yield: 3 ½ cups (840 ml) (14 servings)

1 cup (240 ml) water

1 Tablespoon fresh lemon juice

1 ½ cups (210 g) frozen unsweetened raspberries,
partially thawed

1 ½ cups (150 g) frozen unsweetened strawberries,
partially thawed

1 cup (155 g) frozen unsweetened blueberries,
partially thawed

¾ cup (150 g) granulated sugar

1. Place all ingredients into the Vitamix container in the order
   listed and secure lid.

2. Select Variable 1.

3. Switch machine to Start and slowly increase speed to Variable 10.

4. Blend for 3 minutes, using the tamper to press the ingredients into the blades.

Nutritional Information

Amount Per Serving: *Calories 60, Total Fat 0g, Saturated Fat 0g, Cholesterol 0mg,
Sodium 0mg, Total Carbohydrate 15g, Dietary Fiber 1g, Sugars 13g, Protein 0g*

Vegan   **Vegetarian**   **Dairy-free**   **Gluten-free**

Powdered Sugar

Preparation: 5 minutes | ***Processing:*** 40 seconds | ***Yield:*** 2 cups (480 ml) (96 servings)

1 ½ cups (300 g) granulated sugar

1 Tablespoon cornstarch

1. Place sugar into the Vitamix container and secure lid.

2. Select Variable 1.

3. Switch machine to Start and slowly increase speed to Variable 10.

4. Blend for 30 seconds. Reduce speed to Variable 3 and remove lid plug.

5. Add cornstarch through the lid plug opening and replace lid plug.

6. Slowly increase speed to Variable 10. Blend an additional 10 seconds.

Nutritional Information

Amount Per 1 teaspoon Serving: *Calories 10, Total Fat 0g, Saturated Fat 0g, Cholesterol 0mg, Sodium 0mg, Total Carbohydrate 2g, Dietary Fiber 0g, Sugars 2g, Protein 0g*

Vegan   **Vegetarian**   **Dairy-free**   **Gluten-free**

Creamy Butter Frosting

Preparation: 30 minutes | **Processing:** Pulsing
Yield: 4 cups (960 ml) (32 servings)

½ cup (114 g) unsalted butter, softened
at room temperature for 30 minutes

1 teaspoon vanilla extract

Dash of salt

4 cups (590 g) powdered sugar

¼ cup (60 ml) heavy whipping cream

2–4 Tablespoons (30–60 ml) water

1. Place all ingredients into the Vitamix container in the order
   listed and secure lid.

2. Select Variable 6.

3. Pulse 30 to 60 times, stopping to scrape down the sides of the container
   with a spatula until well blended, adding additional water if needed.

Nutritional Information

Amount Per 2 Tablespoon (30 ml) Serving: *Calories 90, Total Fat 3.5g, Saturated Fat 2.5g,
Cholesterol 10mg, Sodium 0mg, Total Carbohydrate 15g, Dietary Fiber 0g, Sugars 15g, Protein 0g*

Vegetarian **Gluten-free**

Chef's Note

Use this delicious *frosting
on a number of breads
and desserts, such as
Carrot Raisin Muffins (see
Breakfasts) and Brown
Sugar Surprise Cupcakes
(see Desserts).*

Whipped Cream

Preparation: 10 minutes | ***Processing:*** 45 seconds – 1 minute | ***Yield:*** 2 cups (480 ml) (16 servings)

2 cups (480 ml) heavy whipping cream, cold

1. Place cream into the Vitamix container and secure lid.

2. Select Variable 1.

3. Switch machine to Start and slowly increase speed to Variable 10.

4. Blend for 45 seconds to 1 minute or until cream becomes firm and whipped.

Nutritional Information

Amount Per 2 Tablespoon (30 g) Serving: *Calories 100, Total Fat 11g, Saturated Fat 7g, Cholesterol 40mg, Sodium 10mg, Total Carbohydrate 1g, Dietary Fiber 0g, Sugars 0g, Protein 1g*

Vegetarian

Gluten-free

Chocolate Orange Fondue

Preparation: 20 minutes | **Processing:** 4 minutes 40 seconds
Yield: 2 ¼ cups (540 ml) (18 servings)

1 cup (240 ml) heavy whipping cream

2 teaspoons grated orange peel

8 ounces (227 g) semisweet baking chocolate, chopped

3 Tablespoons (45 ml) Grand Marnier

1. Place cream, orange peel, and chocolate into the Vitamix container in the order listed and secure lid.

2. Select Variable 1.

3. Switch machine to Start and slowly increase speed to Variable 10.

4. Blend for 4 minutes 30 seconds.

5. Reduce speed to Variable 1 and remove lid plug. Drizzle Grand Marnier through the lid plug opening. Blend an additional 10 seconds.

6. Pour into a fondue pot and serve.

Nutritional Information

Amount Per 2 Tablespoon (30 ml) Serving: *Calories 130, Total Fat 10g, Saturated Fat 6g, Cholesterol 10mg, Sodium 5mg, Total Carbohydrate 8g, Dietary Fiber 6g, Sugars 6g, Protein 1g*

Vegetarian   Gluten-free

Index

Vegan　　**Vegetarian**　　**Raw**　　**Dairy-free**　　**Gluten-free**

VEGAN

VEGETARIAN

RAW

Beverages

Breakfasts

Appetizers

DAIRY-FREE

Beverages

Cocktails

Breakfasts

Soups

Appetizers

Dressings & Marinades

GLUTEN-FREE